Dagger of Black Eyes in My Heart

Dagger of Black Eyes in My Heart

Little Diary of Love

HIRA LAL

RESOURCE *Publications* • Eugene, Oregon

DAGGER OF BLACK EYES IN MY HEART
Little Diary of Love

Resource Publications
An Imprint of Wipf and Stock Publishers
199 W. 8th Ave., Suite 3
Eugene, OR 97401

www.wipfandstock.com

PAPERBACK ISBN: 979-8-3852-1118-0
HARDCOVER ISBN: 979-8-3852-1119-7
EBOOK ISBN: 979-8-3852-1120-3

04/29/24

Contents

1. Dream of golden eyes girl

As soon as the golden eyes of
The evening fell on me.
My agony heart began to sink in
The boundless ocean with drops of love.

Then your memory flies like a sparrow
And sits on the eyelids of my dreams.
Then I began to feel that the earth was far away and the sky was
   near to me.

Still I think of you with a loving heart
I love you differently, a spiritual love
But In some corner of my beloved's heart,
The feeling of love is bothering her too.

I know that your wisdom will provide greenery
To my withering hopes in my wane life.
As with the touch of the sun's rays scatter in
Whole garden fragrance hidden in the flowers.

When you are away from me,
I feel like a stranger in this crowd of the world.
When you are beside me,
I feel like a tree standing quietly on the bank of a flowing river.

Maybe it's one o'clock in the night
A blurred black light was spread
In the arms of the blue sky. But still,
My eyes are stable on her dreams like black eyes of tonight.

12.10 AM/09/02/2024

Ask my pain from a night

How much I have love for you?
I wish you must assess my love ways.

Please called up any one night,
Lonely it knows how far I strive for love.

When night would expose you,
Who'll come forward along with my torments.

The night is wake up whole night,
Along with my open eyes.

My eyes go through deserted nights,
but night remains settled upon my eyelids.

When My sight reach on myriad stars,
Then cold wind pierces my sight of altitude.

At times I feel numb in such darkest night,
Sometimes night probes into my mourn.

Desert's night seems to stretch around me,
But my eyes remain twitching at my beloved's black eyes.

Whose brighten push my eyes towards the deep darkness,
Then a tender dark fills in my sight.

Alone night knows my agony sore,
My heart beat can be heard on such a night.

When a silence is posed in the lap of night. Then, no one is
  around me who could befriend my suffering soul.

Lonely the darkest night, who sheltered me,
Who consoles me from sorrow in her silent lap. Like a friend.

11.04 AM 3/09/2022/

2. I never do but ever do

Although I am flawlessly,
But my eyes may be of fault,

Please study, it's not my fault that I love you so much.
Maybe my heart is to be wrong for such a deed.

Although I don't like your accent,
But what can I do, my ears yearn for your melodious words.

Even I don't want to chase you
But what can I do, my feet don't stop me from following you.

I don't even want to see you,
But my eyes never overlooked your black-eyes.

Even I don't want to see your raiment,
But I keep looking at the hidden soul in it.

I don't even want to ask you about my love,
But the empty yard of my heart keeps waiting for your feet.

I never want to think about you
But what can i do, my mind doesn't want to be free from your
memories,

I don't want to express my love to anyone,
But what shall I do now that my pen keeps murmuring about my
love.

Even though I have hidden my love in the bottom of my heart,
But my poems are ballads of my love that divulges without telling
me.

11.35 PM 20/08/2022

3. I am following thee as if

You are deep in my heart,
Like the roots of a banyan tree on earth.

You are as dear to me,
As the moon loves her light,

My heart chants your name,
As it beats with your name.

My soul is bent upon thee,
Like a palm tree leaning towards the sea.

My thoughts travel fast to you,
As snow water flows from the mountain to the river.

My heart is drowned in your love,
Like a plateau in the sea.

My feet strives to move towards you,
Like the water of the river to the sea

My arms are always open to you,
As the meadows are open to rain.

My eyes are all the time set on your face,
As the sky always looks down on the earth.

My gaze met with your black-eyes,
As if the milky rays of the moon with the black night.

I seek your innocent face,
Like shade in the hot sun,

My pen keeps analysing your beauty,
As the clouds do on the evergreen mountain.

Longer path of my love is eating away at my breath along even
Your footprints, That's why I am unable to have you.

Rather, this quiet path is silently becoming my pageant,
And surreptitiously stumbling at my feet.

No one ever sees me stop like a tireless traveller.
Rather my steps will keep going to meet you.

11.05pm 28/08/2022

4. Garland of my love dreams

Even though now I'm with you,
But you don't reverence me,
But when I'll away by everlastingly,
When encircled you by recollections,
You will remorse like fish in mud,

I'm fed up of the stressing life here,
Nobody's heart streams of compassion
If I have reliance from you,
Then you are also habitat in that street,
Where no have condolence with one another.

This life is excessively short,
Whose days are too less to even think about counting,
But even the quiet yard of your
Black-eyes doesn't allow me to rest,
Now I plunk down in the shelter of my hope.

Everything I could ever hope for with you have crumbled
That have scattered on the ways of my life,
Yet I want to make a Garland of
These busted dreams,
That I need to place in your neck,

Whenever you will stoop down,
Even this rosary will bow with weight,
Then the gong of dreams cast in
This garland will be heard,
Thus echo of my love will stay in your life.

3.20 Pm 8/7/2023

5. Verdant love

I have dropped in your love,
The fence of your beguiling has confined my body,
I am creeping in your love like a silent worm.

Don't open my fortune book,
Although it's more extended than my life,
But all these pages are without words.

My dreams are falling apart like leaves,
But I still stand like a bald tree,
Since time has passed like a season.

When I had met you one day through my dream,
I put my arms around you and hugged firmly,
Then, I didn't open my eyes for fear of being isolated from you.

Now my worry is streaming in your chuckling,
As the gloom of the mountains flows into the river,
But her black eyes aren't worried about my concern.

10.45 PM 19/10/2023

6. Rain brought us together

Water is pouring down the streets
And heading toward my beloved's village
As it rains heavily.
I intended to see my beloved.

However, rainstorm making obstruction on my way,
I haven't any option to passes on my message,
So, I made a paper boat
And left it in the streaming water.

A picture of black eyes had imposed on it,
When the boat arrived at in dearest's lane,
Where darling was sitting alongside
Her lover remembrance in her entryway,

When the boat was passing before her,
Her found the boat extremely gorgeous,
As soon as she caught the boat,
she too got drenched with rain,

She knew for sure that
This boat was sent to me
By her lover when she saw
A stamped of her black eyes upon it.

She was stampede cheerfully inside and she rush.
She came to meet me in the showering rainfall.
when I embraced her fastly, She also wet me too with her love
I expressed gratitude toward the downpour that brought us
    together.

11.28am 09/08/2022

7. A story behind my eyes

A pair of black eyes are hidden
Behind of my eyes,
Only my untired eyes can unfold it's tale,
How long I've been looking from

Rays of your eyes are immersed in my eyes,
As if water of rain merged into desert's sand,
I am sailing on my love way
As if water on the drowned ways,

The reflection of thoughts is flowing out,
Which is absorbed in the bosom of your black eyes,
I feel like I'm getting lonely don't know why,
Who is gradually losing me in a love mystery.

If my eyes were talking,
That could expose the silence of my love,
Would you probe my lying smile?
And Tell off your black-eyes so as to console.

Only your eyes could gaze
The trouble of my eyes well-off,
Please inhabit my eyes,
And strive with a smile to deliver my life.

Even if you hear my laughter every day
But why don't you strive to look into
But if you look carefully, Behind this smile,
Then a pile of dry pain will appear.

Now finish my wait and
Give up your stubbornness
Let your black eyes feel a pain

About this dying soul.

11.23pm 11/09/2022

8. Endorse of love lamp

I am a burning lamp,
Whose kindle of light is burning with the fire of desire,
It is swinging in the moving air,

Without prop, this light is waking up,
Still it has been raging unabated,
As he swings it seems as if he is calling to some holy spirit,

A black-eyes soul like the darkest night watching it,
She can save this light but no strive is being made,
Maybe she is waiting for thy to extinguished,

The sky is overcast with the light of twinkling stars,
Who is liken with thy light,
Rather, it seems to be moving away from thee,

An unfortunate cold breeze is blowing around it.
Now movement of night's sight drags down thy flame,
As snowball seems to be falling into the midst of a burning
volcano.

It seems as if no one is showing any mercy
And all winds, stars, night wants to extinguish thy light,
In this way, now you stay awake by staying on the endorse of lord.

4.04 12/08/2022

9. Deserted way of black eyes

Still did not stop my steps
Even though are very tired,
Even though I'm drenched in sweat
And summer is in full swing,

My eyes are penetrating the desert way like a butterfly,
Nobody is noticeable from a distance on that hot sand
Still my eyes are looking far away penetrating the intensity
The distance seems to be endless.

However I tirelessly search for my cherish, Like a thirsty camel
    looking for water.
But, it is extremely challenging to achieve unseen objectives,
Like my heart is not giving up,

After many miles a tree saw,
Whose shade is stretch on the way, My mind didn't stay without
    rejoice,
its cool shadow, who kissed my scorch feet,

A little voice touchdown my mind,
Who was able to fascinate my sight
a cute little squirrel was checking up to me,
I am going to ask about my status symbol.

"You're looking for someone," she said quickly
I smiled a little and said yes,
Then he completed his answer,
she has seen a charming girl go,

But i don't have recognized her,
Only a remind her delightful eyes,
Who are black eyes like black clouds,
Go rapidly and stroll with her forever to death.

12.15PM 17/04/2023

10. Zoar of god

As soon as she slapped me
My face turned blue.
I got angry and inquired as to why she slapped me.
Her anger spoke.

Why are you looking at me
Without blinking an eyes? from a long time.
Without a second thought, I said
I think you are very handsome.

However, I'm not seeing you,
Rather,I am seeing that God in you.
How beautiful will he himself be who made you?
So your form was making me see God.

Now i got irate on god
Because of which I got slapped
And asked to God,
"Would you take My revenge from black eyes?"

Who has beaten me
To see your artistry.
Please stop making such beautiful idols,
If you won't take my vengeance.

10.30 PM 21/03/2019

11. How many paths.

I don't know, How to find out and
Where are your hometown,
Where you're lived,
There are many ways on my love path,

All paths seemed to gentle
But when I set off my love journey
It seems rough roads are dark and long.
So I am in a dilemma, which path should I choose?

I am thinking about finite goal of love
How many paths it has, No one right seems
All disasters go to black-eyes way.
To whom i am pursuing, Nothing else.

If i go on these paths by individual
Perhaps these path will be eaten my life,
So i am afraid of the flawed path
And how to find exact by optionally.

I wish someone were here,
Who could remove my wanderings,
So someone come and
Show me the right path.

11.40 PM 12/07/2023

12. Face Of White Rose

A look falls on shocking face like white rose
Leaves of whose sparkled while the day,
Grinning Comes out like the incense
Cheeks feel like delicate leaves of white rose And pits come up
   like the dew drops put in Rose's heart.

Her face pulls in like the mien of beautiful hills,
Her gait set forth like peacocks in rainfall,
White dress makes her look like a white butterfly on a milky rose
Black hair comely as black caterpillar on milky rose
Her wonderful voice sounds like the sweet voice of a cuckoo
   echoing in the valley.

Her glossy bear out her belle
Her sheer soul has no allow of cosmetics, Nature set up break
   even point on her beauty,
Her black eyes come forward to her lover who confirms her
   beauty internally too,
Reality itself commends her form by a fair one.

No allow of any stranger come in,
Who keep in true love with her true lover,
Not a little beguile on her heart's backyard,
Sans her aims people commends her beauty,
She gleam as diamond among other glitters,

9.52pm June (20/06/2019)

13. Hidden love of black eyes under darkness

I loved with black eyes,
This clay lamp in my heart is lit regularly,
Whose oil never runs out,
Even though my nights sleep is stealing
But still I am getting psychological pleasure.

Whose smoke is blackening my soul
Yet, it's hot lit permits no outsider to approach,
My feelings are whirling around its warmth,
The intense rays of the sun are also avoiding falling on it,
Drizzling of this never let to dry eternal happiness,

Gentle dark is also sitting somewhere far off,
Many birds are also waking up in its light,
Many ants are also sitting in its shelter,
But I think the love of black eyes is hidden
In the darkness under this lamp,
Which doesn't appear to me even in the light.

1.45pm February (17/02/2020)

14. Oh wind . . . You run away with me

Oh wind, please you run away with me,
My way is very lonely,
I have no company with me,
I still have a long way to go.

If you will walk with me,
Maybe my breath will also continue,
If you don't walk with me,
Then my breath will also fall apart in my path.

Thus the journey of my love will be incomplete, But the path to
     my destination will not end.
But eyes of my destination will wait my way,
But I will not be there.

I will be grateful to you.
Please make off along with me
And get along with me to that place.
Where dwells my beloved with black eyes.

You can leave me at the door of black eyes And you can come
     back.
Thus by your grace I can Reach
To the floor of my lover.

00.31 19/07/2023

15. Never ever black, But she has

You just like black dresses. I know,
Then why do you want to stay away from my black color?

Why do you irate from my black color?
Even though your mobile with black cover stays in your grasp
    mostly.

Why do you like to stay away from my black color?
Then why are you fascinated by the gleam of your black hair?

Why you apprehensive from my black skin,
While your white fingers never tire with your black laptop.

Why don't you consider my black color, Whereas you choice
    study at black night,

Why don't you hold my black hands,
While your hand never tired on blackBerry,

Why don't you wish to see my black color,
But you never are tired of my black letter poetry.

Why don't you like my black color ?
While your black eyes are preferred by me.

11.20pm September (05/09/2021)

16. Oh Black Clouds...

Oh black clouds, oh black clouds,
Where have you come from?
Why are you alone coming?
Your black rays deluded of black eyes
That mingled into thinking of mud
Oh black clouds, oh black clouds,

Oh black clouds, oh black clouds,
Let me know your location
l think, You are apparently from her country,
Your rays pampering on me like my beloved
Rather deemed me staying like your friend
Oh black clouds, oh black clouds,

Oh black clouds, oh black clouds,
Don't neglect me till the destination,
Let me ablution under your shade,
Let me play hide and seek with your rays,
Please carry me toward my beloved's country,
Oh black clouds, oh black clouds.

9.19pm April (29/04/2022)

17. Why you're not now

Why don't you stand by me now
Instead of future,
Why don't you decide my love now
Instead of pending,
Why don't you probe my love ways
Instead of observe,
Why don't you test my love emotion
Instead of feeling
Why don't you read my poem yourself
Instead of listening,
Why you don't talk me yourself
Instead of consign letter,
Why you don't listen my words
Instead of reading,
Why have you disdain for me
Instead of loving,
Why do you observe by your brain
Instead of seeing by your black eyes,
Why are you still silent for my love
Instead of revealing to me,
Why do you sleep at night
Instead of awake along me,

9.40PM 18/12/1019

18. Black dress of black-eyes

A look of black eyes fell upon me,
It felt as if a storm had broken out,
That blocked the path of my eyes
Everything seemed to disappear,

The storm was swaying fastly
Near which I was passing
He grabs my arms and dragged out,
Even though I'm making noise to escape.

My heart became numb with dread,
Since this was going on in obscurity
The flying dust was likewise go inside me,
My eyes are unable to see anything,

Her pride piles are high,
Dirt is spread even in the yard of the her heart
There is no light of the sun of mercy in its yard,
Whose graciousness can be expected.

However, I additionally like your black dress, Who is set on
    ending my life
If it's not too much trouble, quit wearing this dress,
Also, save my life.

7.35Am 13 july 2022

19. You're...

You are a vacation spot
Where I spent a few days.
I will never forget
How happy I was there.

You are a grave
Wherein my lifeless body lies
My distresses and sentiments are buried
In its soil.

You're a wizard
Whose magic approached
On my heart courtyard
Who is flying like the wind.

You're a needle of
My heart's watch.
Who beats every second
In my heart.

You are a mine
Of loving thoughts
Which my heart never
Weary of reading.

You are such an endure
In whose lap
my tongue is sitting
In the bosom of silence.

You're like a Goddess
Name whom I chant Over and Over
Like heart beats.
And my mind long for visions

3.53pm 09/08/2022

20. The admire of black eyes

I come up your reverence and awe
I honour your chaffer tricks,
I consider your innocent face,
Yet why are you arrogant with me?

My open arms welcome your blossom way,
My transparent heart beats only for you,
My imagination kiss your delicate Palms,
Anyway I seek after till the finish of your quiet prosper,

Your irate words seems me flowers,
These blooms on the embankment of my heart.
I would like to walk with you as a shadow,
I don't want to leave you alone on any path.

I don't want to leave you alone on bed,
I would like to Clutches you in my arms,
I will keep you content in my bosom forever,
My hands raising always to help you,

12.19AM 20/10/2020

21. Holi of black colour

Holi came, Holi came
Brought many colours,
Reflected by affection,
And painted all faces along the way

Various flavours to each one,
Difficult to options them,
Nature colour also dispersion,
Merry networks grow on by affection.

Love loaded with colours,
Whose felicity extend on minds,
Lay off the gap of deprived love
Zeal boosts the career of love,

All hearts are looking colourful
Whose badges represent love,
Every souls dive into colorful lake
Sun rays also dissolve into holi's colour.

Soul of water drenched also
Among various colors of sparkle.
But my heart is stay absorbed
In the black color of black eyes.

But people have afraid of black color,
As the souls of the dead are black,
But l am painted by black colour,
Whose tint has sketch the yard of my heart.

March (16/03/2022)

Holi (Means Indian festival on which day people play with
    different types colours by application on friends faces)

22. If you say.....

If you say you love the rain
In this way you ignored my mud cottage
If you say you love the sun,
Then, You overlooked my diligent effort under The beams of sun,

If you say you love storm,
But You don't analyse my cycling journey toward your way.
If you say you love night,
But You don't think about my eyes
Who awoke the whole night in your memory.

If you say you love your milky colour,
But Then you forget your stunning black-eyes,
If you say you love the ocean's pearls.
It means You don't care about your whitish Teeth as much as a
pearl.

If you say you love my poetry,
Why don't you consider my affection sentiments,
Which in every case expresses itself on you.
I'm afraid of your love commitment
Because you've said you love me now.

10.36pm 18/08/2022

23. Why am I not in your world? whereas you're

Why are you scowl on me,
I know I'm used to your ways,
Accept me from within and not from without,
Even you don't know that i am pinned onto you from within,

I am not a dwells of your world,
But still I keep your black eyes in my heart,
Don't think of me as a Stranger,
But i don't know how i fell in your love,

People say a many times,
Who dies early, They become stars,
How many stars are in the sky,
How will you find me or I you? If we will..

If I am not a part of your world,
Then, How are you a part of my world?
Yet you tell me the way
how I can belong to your world,

Please marry me, Perhaps
I would become a part of your world,
Then our world will merge into one frame. And all the differences
   will disappear.

25/07/2023 11.20, Tuesday

24. I'll want you until end

I always remember you,
I need you generally,
I love you until the end of time,
Any place you live,

When will the time come?
Who will unite us
I will anticipate you,
Eyes will stays on your way,

I will show restraint,
I'll never end your waiting,
Until you get me,
My life will sit down on strike for you.

My each breath will come,
With blinking of black-eyes,
My final gasp willn't leave me
Without your cherished memory.

My arms will be open eternity,
Who need you embrace of all time,
My heart beats
You can hear my heartbeat's grief.

12.30 19/02/2022

25. My life wish

I wish,
You'd look my eyes way
Like me As
I am seeing your black eyes,

Then,
You can see
The love reflected
In my eyes,

I wish,
You glance toward me
As I looking for your presence
On my way,

Then,
You will consider
What a long patience is on
The path of affection.

I wish,
Just as l want you,
You want me
Same likewise.

Then,
You'll know
What is a pain
In love,

I wish,
I will keep on want you ever,
Even though
You will keep on disregard me,

Thus,
You are squandering my exertion,
Thus you're relentless,
Yet I will always be faithful to you in my life.

3.05 pm 30-07-2022

26. You are the rose yourself

You resemble a rose
Whenever I pass by you
Your lovely scent draws me
To you like a beetle.

Which brings joy to my desert heart
Which becomes hustle in my thoughts
Seeing you, the rose remains in my hand
My opinion also fell into thoughts.

I have a rose in my hand for you
But how, I give it to you?
Because you are like roses
Then how can I give you a rose?

I have a rose in my hand for you,
But how do I give it to you?
Since you yourself are like a rose,
Then, how might I give you a rose to rose.

Your black eyes can see distinctly,
The reflection of your rose face is visible in my eyes,
You can now independently determine,
Who can give a rose to a rose?

9.30 PM 06/07/2021

27. If you're outside & Then who is inside

Who is calling me in my heart
Who r u?
You're inner my heart
Then who are you outside?

I am looking from outside,
Sometimes I try to groping towards crowd
When I go to the crowd and stand
Then I tirelessly try to find black eyes there.

Occasionally when I meet my beloved
Then I get restless, as
I feel some soul is digging
With a dagger at my heart.

Then my thinking also falls
into my thinking,
If a beloved with black eyes is outside,
Who is stabbing my heart inside?

Having troubling does not allow me
To ask my restless,
Don't understand anything what to do
Who is outside or who is inside.

11.43PM 12/03/2023

28. Unusual day

No crowd near me
There is no desire around me
But crowds of people have
Seen the wishes flying past me.

While numerous companions,
Relationships and family,
Who could adequate.
But nobody was aware of my day.

Just empty outlooks are
Viewing their way.
Who could be gratified for mine.
But it seemed like a lonely tree.

I bought some chocolate rather than
A hustle in order to achieve my goals.
But I didn't see that
There was no expectation ahead of me.

When l begin to hand out
A crowd appeared ahead,
That contain numerous children,
Who seized chocolate from mine.

Many wishes are being conferred
Although they don't know my birthday.
However happy birthday wishes play a role On bare paths who
    are waiting since morning.

An enduring expectation broke out
While an auspicious soul doesn't come here,
Whose black eyes full of best wishes.
But my enduring hope seemed like a staying skeleton.

10.45pm 17/03/2023

29. Endless desire of life

My desire will be never ending
To get you until my life,
Even if you keep run away from me
But I will follow you tirelessly

I will also cry out to God
who made you, To make you mine forever.
I will also ask your parents,
who borne you. To deliver you mine forever.

You can get tired
Of running away from me,
But I'll never get tired of following you,
Earlier blinking of your black-eyes you'll find me before you.

Then I will not care about myself,
Then be health or mind,
Whether the feet are bare or not,
Then the paths are clear or rough.

Even if my journey is never ending,
But I will keep myself going
As long as my body will not unable
Or until I find my girlfriend.

10:00 PM 19/10/2023

30. My Best Kite

Although, i am the owner of many kites,
But it is challenging to pick which one to fly.
Each one kite might want to roaming in sky,
All kites are thrilled about the festival of lohri.

Lohri give them an opportunity to floating,
Every kite is take off to dive into the sky,
Every kite is ready to strolling on this road,
No turn points are found in the yard of the sky.

Entire day l took part in flying kites,
The number of kites I have was diminishing,
Since the string of my kites were cutting by other kiter,
So, at last I had flipped out a black-eyed kite.

I gave a chance to this black-eyed kite,
Sky is full of different variety kites,
Still, my kite affirms distinguished identification in sky,
As black eyes are seeing to the mien of earth.

This kite is identifiable among fair of kites,
Which is measuring all altitude of my love life,
So,Knowing all this I decided not to fly it,
Since it figure out sensations of my heart,

So, l have afraid in my mind to lost it,
Like my other kites who left me alone,
But l would like to keep it into my heart,
To whom I will share the love of my whole life.

10.45pm January (12/01/2022)

31. I think ever

I use to afraid that
You may not be lost
From me in life.
How'll I find you from
A crowded world anyway?

when I am going to sleep
Then you aren't with me
And when l wake up
You're not on the bed sheet.
Then my heart falls into depression.

I want to avoid my mistakes by
The company of your black eyes
So that it can be truthfully,
But you aren't along with me due to which
My tongue has got freedom from falsity.

I have nobody, with whom
I can share my confidential life,
With whom I would
A traveller of life
Throughout my life.

12.05 pm 12/08/2022

32. If I were a cloud

If I were a cloud,
I could wandering on the sky's road,
Her courtyard could save from sunny,
Who burning her heart steadily,

I could blend in with her black eyes,
Whose contrast can never be separated. Every corner of our path
   is polished black. The only ray of hope is that we live together
   on a black deck.

The drops of rains will be pour down,
On her desolate way,
So her feet could save from burning
To her journey to my love way.

The chirping might be listen
On her courtyard,
While different Birds do rapture,
Humidity of mine will touchdown their feathers,

Raindrops of mine would like
To wash away her black curly hair
As she would swirl in the pouring rain.
Whose drench will hug her auspicious soul.

11.48 AM 03/09/2022

33. Oh . . . Listen me

Oh gracious . . . wind listen my talk,
Try not to blow the tresses of my affection,
Blow away my worn garments though.

Oh . . . sun, Please listen to me.
Don't touch my beloved with your golden fiery rays.
Even burn my flesh although.

Oh . . . rain of sorrow, Pay attention to me. Don't fall on my love's
  fate,
Even if you break down like a mountain on my fate.

Oh.. Gracious, Mother earth listen to me,
Grasp your child's distress,
Give me the love of my love,

Oh...kindhearted, Night infer my silence,
Tie up the recollections of my love with my cot,
So that my desolate mind keeps playing with them,

Oh.. passers, hear my crying,
Fathom my pleas throughout the falling tears,
Carry my message to my beloved,

Oh.. Flickering stars, Let me know a mystery,
How did you teach black-eyes to hide her sight,
As if your sight hides in the sky during the day.

02/01/2023 1.30 pm

34. Jingle of glory

If I write the applaud of your black eyes
Then my pen goes to shame
Your glory is longer than the river Nile,
The ink of my pen runs out while writing.

If I talk about beauty,
Then your beauty is the most beautiful
Before whose beauty the moon fades.
It also more than the beauty of any Miss Universe of the world.

Your dark hair is more lovely than
An evergreen mountain.
The night of your black eyes is longer
And darker than the night of the Amazon forest.

I feel your aloneness
Like the streaming of amazon river.
Even if she comes across the beautiful Amazon trees, she goes on
    ahead regardless.

If I talk about your temperament
Then I feel like an unsolvable math
When my feelings demolished to solve it
Then I feel a chemistry reaction in my body.

12.45 PM 09/01/2024

35. My lust will never die to have you

If you'll be not meet me
In this life,
Nevertheless in spite of that
I persisted to have thee in the next life.

Let me see your face too
In my future dreams,
And my dreams will never be withered
At any moment in my ongoing life.

Although my life has brought me
Many benefits and rewards,
And my hands are filled with blessings,
But they are devoid of your touched,

When I see other lovers bereft of
Their love and their ongoing lives crumbled,
I take comfort in thinking that one more ruined Life won't make
a difference in the world.

Don't have to afraid on the way of love,
Albeit the distress of affection is coming all over,
However I stay broken without you in your memory.
Even though you are not with me, you have turned into a breath
of my life.

5.26 Pm 20/08/2022

36. Quiz of black-eyes

My faith has been uprooted
Like a gust of wind has uprooted a nest.
I stroll around looking for a way in the sand,
Sometimes I walk around looking
For the shadow of the sun.

Someone asked me
Whereabouts black eyes location.
I told them that she lives,
Where even the wind passes
Through halting its breath.

During the day
Beams of sun pampering with her.
And at night the moon and
Millions of stars keep playing with her.
Darkest also vanishes by visible her.

My heart has not changed still
Like the heart of a river who wants to meet the ocean.
Who want you by constantly,
But your zeal is fading to meet me
Like a river of desert to meet the ocean.

11.45 PM 14/11/2023

37. Hear the sorrowful soul

If you knock on my heart,
You'll hear the cry of the suffering soul,
If your look carefully,
It seems that this soul has lost love,

If you listen to it carefully,
This grief soul is chanting the name of some spirit,
If you consider her pronounce words,
It seems like an articulation of black eyes.

If you want to free this soul,
Cast your black eye magic on it,
Because he is buried under the stamp of black eyes.
But If you analyse from the core of your heart,

Hold his hands in your hands,
Put it on your shoulder and embrace it firmly,
When two souls will become one life,
In this way life will become heaven on earth,

If you save a life,
You will get it back,
In this manner you will turn into
A motivation for the approaching age,

11.45PM 12/09/2021

38. Change is the law of the universe

If, weather changes,
If, season changes,
If, days changes,
If, air direction changes,
If, water of rivers changes,
If, mother earth revolving,
If, shade changes,
If, rays changes,
If, glaciers changes,
If, fragrance changes,
If, black night changes,
If, our age changes
If, people changes
Then why not your black eyes?
The direction of which can change in any direction.

10.27pm may (25/05/2022)

39. A school of heart

A gorgeous soul has come beautifully
Who is wearing a black dress,
Gracefully like a straight waterfall
Who is falling from a black mountain.

My eyes didn't disallow her,
Who abide by their duty,
Who fascinate from her glory
I get it into my heart patio.

Who came a calm visit to school
It is exist in my heart courtyard,
No students present Here,
Except the blissfully hopes,

She took admission,
Without anyone permission,
She choice a topic
As "love poetries" on her black-eyes,

No charges pay here
So she is spreading her love with next to no cost
Only is a straight way learning here
From eyes to eyes reading feelings.

Therefore, many highlights of walking
On the path of love are preached in it.
Whose irrigation through the canal of the eyes is done
Till the cultivation of the heart's love.

7.40 Am 13 July 2022

40. Unforgettable moment

I always remember our most memorable gathering,
When quiet talked was carried on,
Our eyes locked in one another,
Our steps were going together by aligning.

To the extent that long way was getting less as well,
Tender evening fell around us
After this, the night also came,
Moonlight too was tickling us.

Even though our eyes weren't wear out,
My heart was beating quickly
Because I was with
The heaven spirit's black eyes.

Might be our souls would have desires,
To stay in lap of such delightful time,
Who was exploring two hearts
Feelings that were buried a long time ago.

10.10pm 29/07/2022

41. Let us make a love forever

Let our emotion inscribe on
Blank pages of my heart's book,
Let me accomplished our love script,
Let the flow of emotions to my heart.

Let our love a part of library
Lonely a place where to stay forever
Our love would remain refresh wherein
When our love would probe on by new lovers.

Let your sight to journey
Towards my aloneness route of love,
Let your emotions inhabited
Into my heart's deserted home.

Let write down my pen
In lyrics of our love
Let Carry out our love a scrutiny
In stanza to the coming world.

Let born ravishing flowers
Into my heart's desolate track.
Whose scent will reach out to
New lovers that would lead to true love.

Let people guess your black-eyes
At the tricks of your love.
So that people can reconcile
Their feelings with our love.

11.21pm April (27/04/2022)

42. I am dying little by little every day

Why did you leave me
While I have not left you, Now
Every day I am dying a little by little,
As the vine dries up without water,

I keep asking myself about you.
My dream is to spend my life with you.
I want to take all my breaths for you
But your black-eyes are overlooking.

You gave me
A symbol of sorrow and gloom,
Still you are looking for gain And
You hurt me as futile without any reason.

I used to be very nice
These are not my words but of people.
You are also right,
But I don't know why you are doing this.

You drowned me in the midst of life,
Without pity on my little life,
The dagger of Your black eyes pierce my heart every time, when I
  see you.

12/08/2023 11.40

43. But worry remains to become a regret

I know
you don't like me,
I know this too
You're overlooking me every time.
As much as you hate me.
But I don't think you ever think of me,
But it doesn't matter to me,
I loved you, always have and will always love you.
As much as i want you,
Then I will tell you when you become mine,
When the cloudy rain will pour by your black-eyes,
Then one of my words will be feel for Mercy,
As much as I want you
Then you will tell the people by crying.
You will want to meet me then & realised
I want you how much
Then you will have only worry left
As time passed, but
The worry remains to become a regret.

11.17 02/08/2023

44. Draw your breath along with me

I feel like you are an iceberg
From which I keep slipping,
Your beauty seems like a dark shadow
With which I am going backwards,

Your anger cool down me
Like the moon's flame,
Your silence probes into
The darkest night's mystery.

Your nature is flowing me
Like river water.
You are drowned the people like
An ocean wave without caring about anyone.

My memory has vanished
Into your black eyes.
Which can be remembered on
The pleasant daylight when you will meet me.

Your black eyes aren't seeing
My tears as a hungry lion,
As he doesn't see the tears of a deer,
Your longing appears to be wild,

You are erupting like a volcano at my every proposal,
Think of me as the wind,
And draw your breath along with me,
If you want to live a long life.

12.30AM 19/07/2023

45. Colour of black-eyes

As many crowd are brimming with colours here
Who is dyed in different colours
i am also not missed from this mob
Although many colours have been spilled on me too.

But I still didn't feel tanned,
But what happened unexpectedly,
When recall of black-eye merged into my eyes
Then I became a victim of your black-eye.

Every colour looks faded on me
But this black colour dyed my eyes
So all colours of mob seem black to mine
Even if my colour is also black.

Now the holi of water falling too
It looks like rain falling from a black cloud,
This rain has washed away all my colours
But your black eyes' colour didn't go away.

I was feeling alone even in the holi crowd
The Holi crowd was showering colours
Along with water on me, But my inner soul
was absorbed in the black eyes of my love.

The dark shade of holi was slaying my spirit
The warm sun likewise came on the planet
Along with breeze to be a part of holi mob
Who consoled my trembling soul in this crowd.

09/03/2023 (00.16 AM)

46. Dig out carefully a queer story

What do I do with someone?
When you are not with me,
I am crazy about you my love
I don't want to look at
Anyone else's door except your way.
I can't win you and
I can't take you for a price.
what you're for me,
I am unable to tell you
Look into my eyes carefully
Deep dig out here a story
That seems very mysterious,
Even if it is about
A suffering soul in silence.
Your black eyes met me,
Like darkness Storm meet to black night,
Of which I seek nothing
But except desolation.
My face has lost the smile,
Even if you think it is pride.

9.40 PM 30/05/2021

47. City of mystery

What a wonderful your city,
Where l have seen elegance,
What a pleasant fencing around city,
Silence of your city is also befit,

Where blustery night deluded my eyes,
Where fragrance isn't leaving it's confluence,
Where the song of affection is mixing the series of hearts,
Where every step would be like dancing.

Yet, I was unable to see anything appropriately,
Since I couldn't light a lamp of love in my heart.
That could explore the right things in the right place on a
    pleasant night.
Might be your burning lamp will light my attachment lamp as
    well.

However my mind is meandering alone
Since many days hours,
But rambling with aimlessly couldn't beat
My steps in the lanes of such city,

Just two black-eyes gleaming there,
Whose sparkling is piercing my sight,
But I was unable to see her presumptive worth In the absence of
    light,
But she seems to be a divine soul.

10.57 pm 14/08/2022

48. Rose garden of heart

My eyes on feelings,
My heart is sniffing,
My waiting finished,
While rose day came,
Rose plants grown,
On the heart ranch,
What I would like to,
Cultivate on this day.
My eyes is looking on,
Many couples with rose,
Who lovers symbolises,
What a love invitation.
But no one beloved,
Would reach out on,
Garden of my heart,
To jump at red roses.
So, garden of red rose,
Would remain uncouth,
To cultivate such roses,
Put by the next rose day,
The owner of rose garden,
Never avoid such farming,
Wait upon black eyes way,
Who could walk off with.
Hope of ray, never pass
On and welcome to dawn,
Surviving the fading rose,
Scents always, asks for her.
But nature, never allow,
To be immortal anything,
Waiting soul must set forth,
Her love before fading rose.

11.37pm November (12/11/2021)

49. Do you know?

Are you aware?
I love you unimaginable,

Do you have too,
As much as i love you,

Do you count words?
How much is inscribed in poetry towards you?

Don't you measure?
How much blossom are my love ways?

Don't you study my poetry ?
How much love is reflected by my poetry?

Have you ever experienced this?
How quick does my heart beat for you?

Don't you analyse?
How much is my silence worth for you?

Don't you notice?
How much of a gap there is between us while chasing you.

Do you think?
How much exertion is paying to get you?

Are you aware of black eyes ?
How much do my eyes love them?

Provided that this is true,
Pass on them a message of my genuine romance,

11.15AM 19/12/2020

50. Black ocean

As my steps slipped across,
And fell in the black ocean,
Whose origin from black cave,
Seems it is flowing from black eyes.

Black ocean drowned me
With steady flow of visionless way
Many dive are hurdle
To stir my breath.

Water filled into my body
Called out through hands outward
Upto head inhale to water
Only water knows my exertions.

Nobody there,
Except a soul with dark black eyes,
Who hadn't any strive,
Rather the view was being enjoyed.

As soon as my body started to stream,
My spirit couldn't bear this hustle,
that stimulated my reasoning,
What promptly transforms my idea into apprehensive.

But my think thinks nothing possible,
My beloved stands by me forever like a false.
In front of whose, l am pouring into such black ocean,
Now I came to grasp that l drowned that ocean of his black eyes.

10.49pm May (20/05/2022)

54

51. Endless desire of life

My desire will be never ending
To get you until my life,
Even if you keep run away from me
But I will follow you tirelessly.

I will also cry out to God
who made you, To make you mine forever.
I will also ask your parents, who borne you.
To deliver you mine forever.

You can get tired
Of running away from me,
But I'll never get tired of following you,
Earlier blinking of your black-eyes you'll find me before you.

Then I will not care about myself,
Then be health or mind,
Whether the feet are bare or not,
Then the paths are clear or rough.

Even if my journey is never ending,
But I will keep myself going
As long as my body not be able to buried
Or until I find my girlfriend.

10:00 PM 19/10/2023

52. Blessing of the stars

I couldn't sleep last night,
Suddenly a flock of stars came,
They asked me What happened you,
I expressed I am tripped in black-eyes rays.

Who is she? They asked,
When my tireless eyes reflect her image,
They console me,
Many beautiful girls are here like such,

I didn't believe,
They said till morning
We will tell you about
A more beautiful girl than this one.

First their eyes search for her in Asia
Then they go to Europe after they go to America. however
They are unable to find such a Queen girl.

Finally, they go to Australia,
But there is no princess girl.
Then they get tired & feel lost themselves,
Lastly they go to Punjab, the land of India.

As soon as the day broke, they came & said
We have not found anyone else
In the world like this girl who is beautiful, Obedient to her
    parents and charming.

As soon as the day burst up,
Stars were about to disappear,
They blessed me to get my true
And pure love about black eyes soul.

12.55 pm 22/07/2023

53. Helpless stare

By the way, thousands come in your way
But what did you see in me?
Am I not in the crowd of those thousands?
Why did you choose me?

So,
Why do you disfavour me only,
Leaving many others?
It's not justice for me.

But you hate me instead of love
Whereas I love you instead of hate
You must think about this issue
Sometime in your life. What is right and wrong?

Even if you don't love me,
Then tell your memory not to torment me.
What have I lost to you?
Leave such to anger now, and have mercy.

Yes,
I also admit my fault that I love you
From the bottom of my heart,
But what can I do, you are the only girl I like.

Even if, you don't even look at me
I look at you with my helplessness.
Whether your black-eyes know it or not, but Your wisdom knows
    my helpless reality.

10.45PM 07/09/2023

54. Inquire through window

My sight are being satisfy with inner sunshine,
Who penetrated through my cabin window
I felt as if it was sitting in the chair next to me,
With carefully l was watching,

While I was view, there was came another one,
A black cloud was hovering near my window,
lt took the place of sunshine,
It started to get dark in.

As darkness fell, it seemed that some Black-eyed soul was close to
my heart,
Then I looked out the window,
Now my gaze was conversing with him,

Through conversation I now inquired about his city,
Now he started telling me about my beloved,
Who also a resident of his heavenly city,
As her black eyes colour is same like the black cloud,

10:25pm 25/08/2022

55. Don't pride on your beauty

What do you think?
All is here have you,
Or all is stay have you
But nothing stays forever here at all to anyone.

All these in the queue,
Who are asking their turn
Mistime is floating on all way of life,
That will knock down every stir of souls.

Fairs of fairs will be wind up,
Every bright would be blurred,
Each blood would grow old,
Widening of wrinkles is a token of ending life,

No chirping would be listen out tomorrow
The leaves will fall down peacefully
Yard of mother earth would die down by devastate
Rays of desert will get about around us.

Bustle of life would be obscure,
Pleasure would be far away,
Feelings would be gone to be dull,
Nobody will feel out your aloneness,

If, my turn is today in the queue of ending
Your black eyes will also shut up tomorrow,
Each life would withered & dying out,
So don't get on with pride of your beauty,

11.53 pm May (21/05/2022)

56. I want a decision from you too

If she giggle when my poem convey my love,
I would deliver for what seems a valid like forever for her,
I maintain that she should rebuff my wrong doing at each step,

I believe that she should turn into an affection for my life.
If I forgot myself, what did I forget,
I will forget God in her memory

I wish that the tempest of sorrow never hold her
I have become addicted to being faithful to you.
All calls insane me for her,

Anyway I'm attempting to eliminate the veil From her face all
   through the verse,
I expressed your black-eyes all through the statement,

Presently if anybody believes
You should rebuff me or kill me or leave me alive,
So I need to hear a decision from you.

8.30AM 29/01/2022

57. Accustomed of black-eyes

My eyes are not tired
Seeing the black eyes
Even though the mind is tired,
In eternal hope of his love.

Even when I read books
My eyes fall on black letters,
But heed doesn't go to the meaning of these black letters,
Because they only reflect black eyes.

But I am sick of reading books
So it's pointless to hold them,
As if I don't get anything out of them.
Seems a matter of console my minds myself,

My eyes catch a sight of black-eyes,
But nothing ready to consider else anything
Be that as it may, I'm getting destroy into the obscurity of black
    eyes path,
So take by my arm and lead me out of the dark,

1.30 PM 23/07/2021

61

58. I want to be with her forever

A night spent its entire night on my eyelids,
A miserable young lass sat on the threshold of my eyes,
Who had endured silence in her eyes like an idol.
She was disheartened by somebody's memory.

If I probe her silent, many thousands woe have,
If I share her mourn & Remaining breaths would be over too,
If I see tears in her black-eyes,
So it seems as though the downpour is moistening the lap of
mother earth,

Whether she accent her yes or not,
But I'm prepared to alleviate her profound aggravation forever
Although she comes to me or not,
But the dagger of her memory rings in my chest everyday.

Her curly hair falls on my fortune look like a veil,
This veil keeps projecting us as love laden way,
If moonlight shower upon my eyes then her milky face ingests
into my eyes,
If I ask from night about her anguish, it likewise stays quiet.

Wit of mine stand by her till my final gasp,
My eyes touch savour of her torments,
I don't care if she is good or bad,
But I want to be with her forever,

10.23pm 6/09/2022

59. Confess your love with my crush

I love you more than l have,
Whereas
You don't love other than
You do yourself.

Maybe
I am pouring my love
Into the weak hands
Which are unable to hold my love.

My love is rising barefoot to your black eyes, But l slip on your
    eyelids
Still, I don't want to see anyone else
After your black eyes slip through the threshold.

Therefore, appreciate it
If other people can become followers of love And why don't you,
So not be afraid of the cycle of love.

In exchange for my love
Show a little bit of your affection
So that the value of our love fills into one bowl
And sip it gradually alongside me undoubtedly.

11.23 AM 12/08/2022

60. Kinder journey of love

If I couldn't flutter,
But l am running after you,
If I couldn't run,
Then l stroll after you,
If l couldn't walk,
Then i would crawling after you,
If I couldn't crawl,
Then my tune could arrive at on you,
If my tune would hush up,
My body would be melting
By the hottest beams of sun,
Then it will become black clouds of evaporation,
Who are hovering into sky of your black-eyes,
Drops of rain would be fallen afterwards,
These will wash up my skeleton.
Whose flowing will push off my vacantly Skelton Into the
   auspicious water of ganga river,
Water of which will carry on my dreams loaded body to the
   objectiveless destination of my endless journey.

00.13am 07/09/2022

61. Just be aware

Hi.. My dear, are you aware?
You don't have a clue about the reality, I know,
Even though I'm crazy about you to have you,
Maybe only nature knows. Why is there still silence?

Be darling of mine than rival,
Try not to press my sentiments tied with compulsion,
Rather make a mainstay of safe life,
On which stay a prosperous my whole journey of life,

For what reason do you desire to give more agony,
Already life of mine brimming with misery,
There is no room here for other distresses,
Don't despise my soul I am also human,

Stop gleam of outraged by your black-eyes,
That flame burns the valley of my heart,
Please don't destroy this infertile valley,
Instead, plant the green trees by your grace.

Whose greenery will enliven the arid valley,
So that declining love can be restored,
Who might turn into for carrying on with life,
Where I will go through my time on earth joyfully with you.

11.15PM 27/03/2020

62. Exceptional love of mine

I love thee because you have antique visage on the earth,
I love thee because no one else like you,
I love thee with love exceptional,
I love thee with a solitary breath.

I love thee measureless,
Whose has countless width, length & height,
Thus When you out of sight,
My feelings blinks like the tide of ocean,

No one can assess my love as like the profound of pacific ocean,
So I hold overflow love for you in such profundity,
I love you uninhibitedly
Like a meandered butterfly.

I have found out you by losing myself,
I don't want to far you away,
Your black eyes make me crazy about you,
I shall love your black-eyes after death too.

10.45 PM 13/07/2022

63. Soul of Prison

No one is digging out
My buried feelings,
Under the dry rubbish of pain,
That makes me cry in my life.

Usually people see happy faces
But no one is thinking far away from it,
To whom i care
Who wholly neglects me.

Still i am useless
My efforts makes me void
Do you see?
Someone is doing it with intention.

My lonely soul is in prison of sorrow
That dwell into the ocean of black-eyes
Who is tormented by bear such love grief
Who is obsessed with the performed promises.

I cannot flee from such a deep prison
Which sinking in water by gradually
One day this prison will sink into this
Deep black sea with a tormented thirsty soul.

08/09/2023 12.45AM

64. A yellow dress

Like sun i born and die everyday,
I burn every day in the fire
On the rising day, fire tread on me,
whose flames are rising very high,

Barren land of my chest gleam like a cremate,
No seed sprouts in it, Although it gives Warmth to the sprouting
    Flora,
But my born desires would be crushed,

Never dayrise without sun,
Nor does it rain without a dark cloud,
Without rain, the earth never be chilled,
Without wind the leaves of the tree do not move,

The waves of your yellow clothes
Embraced the rays of sun,
Your black eyes got on wet
In the meadows of the dark cloud,

Your trembling heart with yellow flames came
In my warm embrace in the yellow beams of sun.
How can I leave your lonely courage in such Meadows of wheat
    like your yellow dress.

9.45 PM 23/01/2023

65. Lover of lonely alone

Lovers of moonlight are many more here
But why am I a lover of sunshine?
Crowd always a fans of hustle & bustle
But why am I a lover of quietness?

Mostly people like white colours, but
I fan the black colour of black-eyes
Green is the lovely colour of the season
But the colour of my love is black.

Many lovers were in the queue in your youth. But why have I
been in the queue since childhood?
You don't listen my sore of utterance
But why am I absorbing your smile?

All lovers would like to their love swaying through wind,
But why would I like to dandle through the rain?
People always live with their expectations. However I'm living
with trust on you.

12.25Pm 24/08/2022

66. Black-eyes didn't keep their promise

A cruel love, shows me
A soul of black-eyes,
As soon as I saw her,
I fell in love with her.

She deftly dealt with
My every step on the way of love,
As much as it slowed down my pace and Made me forget the way
   to the destination.

When I sat next to the black eyes,
They encouraged me that
The one you are looking for,
I am your destination.

When I posed her my question that
you will uphold me forever,
throughout my life,
She stayed silent.

On my silence,
She promptly answered,
I'm your life and I will cherish you
More than life for the rest of my liveliness.

Hearing this response from her
I chose to consume
My life on earth with her
Without contemplating anything.

Since I have been anguishing
From the aggravation of my life
Since the days fell into worry,
But now she does not regard me.

11.55 pm 11/08/2022

67. Prove me on the love way

Why I love you
For what I find in you,
I experience passionate feelings for you,
Attributable to your black eyes.

Why I love you
I love what I hear out
From your lovely voice
And talk over your words.

Why I love you
For what I feel your emotions
And analyse your loved heart.
Try to feel out my lovely love.

Why I love you
Your every step go away with
Hand in hand with my steps.
Which is the witness of your honesty.

But if I don't love you
You can find out
When l entertain you
Throughout lust, use it in the love way.

I love you or not, You can feel for,
You can prove me anytime
Even if it is the way of love
Or infatuation. And go over into my love.

00.37AM 11/08/2022

71

68. Once you must try to know my love

Why are you angry, oh goodness my beloved ?
I love thee such that will not end when I die too
I too know that you don't love me.
I even know that you discriminate against my caste.

Please inform me of my fault, For what you're hurting me.
Maybe you don't have any idea the amount I love you,
Still I need to let you know my affection,
Don't listen to it even if, kindly, compassionately read these lines.

I also feel that you will overlook my love,
But your black eyes will never forget my true love lines,
Even the world will know my immortal love,
Even if you don't have room for me in your heart,
But the meadow of your eyes are enough,
And regardless of whether you value my love or not, the world
    will.

Let me expose my genuine love,
If you don't mind, your black-eyes can visit on my eyes meadows,
You can smell the fragrance of the garden of love grown on this
    meadow,
Thus you must have understood how I can devastate this garden
    by myself.
Regardless of what you do, you can never pay the expense of my
    affection.

Everything is paid for thought however you are harming me as a
    consideration for my affection.
My heart was like a blank book,
Whatever is passing on this heart is splashing on it,
That is contained in this black-eyes poetry book. you can
    understand if you read such book from the bottom of heart.

10.30PM 08/06/2022

69. Illusion of blinking stars

Endless stars are shimmering,
Whose are floating in the sky,
My eyes are full of with illusion,
That look to be the Black Ocean,

There has been a lot of time spent,
Whose pretty beams blinking steady,
I'm befuddled over and over,
It seemed like they were sitting on a black mountain.

Dark rays are carrying on contiguity,
Towards my eyes alongside wind,
The truth is also push beyond their way,
Because i am habitual of such dark rays,

Such sharp splendid harmed my heart,
Likewise strayed my consideration of brain,
Which looks like the black eyes squinting,
As my dearest's black eyes glimmered.

9.54pm February (28/02/2022)

70. Dark of your Black-eyes

I am walking toward
The darkness in your black-eyes
When I am standing in front of it
Then my thoughts are confronting it.

I am seeing my soul
Captive in the thick branches
Covered with the shadow of sorrow
In which my breaths are anguishing.

Trying to gleam in such blackness
Longing for peace and solitude arisen
Attempting to unchained myself
Whose is very annoying to me.

With a little nod of your head
A calm and serenity rays uplifted into my heart
Today your soul could see that stillness in me
That originated from the fear of your black-eyes dark.

12.45 AM 21/07/2023

71. Distance along our way

I am stayed like a trees
You changed like seasons
I'm sit with the promise yet
you went away without commitments.

My final gasp are anticipating you,
You are leaving me alone in needed,
I am locked in your thinking cage,
But your reasoning is moving on freely,

Revere is exposed from my side,
But all these overlooked by you,
I'm lost looking for you in fair of people,
But God knows what path you have taken.

I am engaging to care you,
But You're not aware with my ways,
I am always do commending you,
You always take on my mocking,

I am lover of your black-eyes,
You don't know my eyes like cat
I am looking the way of you,
As a cat looking for her way for a rat.

3.20pm May (31/05/2022)

72. Washed away my suffering

Heap of suffering on
My head is high,

whose I can't carry
On such weight,

I prayed for god to washed
Away my all suffering,

As soon as I prayed groups of
Black clouds came.

I stood under the clouds & raised my hands And said remove all
my pains.

At the same time
Heavy rain started.

As if the tears were falling
From the black eyes of a black cloud.

Who reflect weight of pain
On my head.

As my weight was getting lighter,
I felt like they were collapsing the pile of pain.

As soon as the rain stopped,
My weight became like flowers,

I welcomed the black eyes
That shed their tears for me.

4.50pm 09/08/2022

73. Please.... Tell Me

I love you to an extreme,
I always admire you,
I avow your beauty,
I concede your demeanour,
I like your style,
I love your arrogance,
I love your voice as well,
I swallow all your wordses,
I hail your future achievement,
I acknowledge your sublime I quette,
I will always remember your bruised black eyes.
I have no grievances against you,
I in every case most welcome your appearance,
I generally keep your picture in my eyes,
I keep looking for the path of your vision,
I keep your spirit like a blooms flower in my heart,
Your name keeps beating in my heart all the time,
Why are you angry with me anyway?

11.47am April (13/04/2022)

74. Nor our night same

When you are sleeping peacefully
But I am awakening then,
When you are having a restful night
While my night is passing by anguish
When your black eyes are dreaming sweet dreams
But my eyes are counting stars then.
When your holi soul rambles aimlessly in heaven,
But my soul keeps stumbling on rugged roads
When your sleep being snortless,
Then my soul is awaking with wheeze,
When your charming body playing with night,
Then my body is keep fighting with night,
When you wake up at dawn,
Then i am still awaking
When you go to implore before God,
Even then I keep immersed in your vision,
when you see the sunshine at sunrise,
Then sun rays see at me with puzzle eyes,
When you engage with your mobile,
Then still my mind is kept allied with your memory.

11.45pm 08/05/2022

75. Best ever your yellow dress

It seems like flames are
Coming out in the rays of the sun.
When you bear a yellow dress,

The yellow dress caresses you
As if the sun's rays are playing
Caresses with the white rose.

As if the sun's rays are blocked by dark
Clouds, As the shine of your black eyes
Looks like this on your yellow suit,

Your swirls hair cover your
Yellow clothes like a black shadow of
Banyan trees mask the rays of the sun.

Your yellow dress suit you perfectly
As the sunny flames are pampering
With ripe wheat.

00.23 AM 19/08/2023

76. Vexed with a street of love

I don't know where to go,
I can't track down a genuine corner for life,
If I get on the impartial street by chance
That street additionally misjudges me.

Every way seems to be false,
No place seems to be true,
No one seems to be telling the truth. Despite their greetings
     there.

Everything appears to be black to me,
Like my beloved's eyes are black.
Whose yard drowned in the darkest,
Whose streets have become faints.

I don't have a clue about a spirit
Who could lead me toward her city
Whose sky is loaded up with mists,
Drops of which downpour will cool my burning head.

I don't know, where l go and
To whom I can go who can look at The torment of my pain.
Where there might be the hope for probe in my lost love.

The glare of my love can be gazed
From my eyes like the radiance Of snow-capped mountains.
As you know eyes never lie like wind.

11.31AM 03/09/2022

77. Why're you these?

I think,
Maybe You haven't response,
For what reason would you say you are so gorgeous?
Which attracts every eye along the way.

Do you know?
From where your perfection came?
That enable you perfect on every single way,
Whose fragrance comes out on your way,

You are not naive
Although many eyes are stuck on your beauty, Still your gait
    never loses its pride.
Who keeps strolling with her self-importance steps.

Why are Your laughs so cute?
Who surrender a best voice
To all audience's ear,
Nobody can keep away from this.

Why do you remain silent?
Since you have divine characteristics,
Maybe you ought to communicate it with euphoria,
You don't grasp anybody and you do it as you would prefer.

Finally I respond to you
That the one who created you has created
You with great devotion and time,
And has endowed you with divine powers that add to your
    beauty,

11.10AM 18/12/2021

78. Immortal love of a short span

Once I was going on deserted road,
But no one was on the way,
who could stand by me,
Except the trees on the banks of way,

As the proofs actually stand yet
Who can bear my witness
One can ask them
They will answer very soon.

As a black eyes girl came on my way,
She confer some time to me,
But I don't know for what?
Maybe to relieve my loneliness,

But the one that she gave me a little span,
I foolishly mistook it was love,
I have kept it salvage to the present day,
Anybody can find it in the vault of my heart.

I now have no idea why this has taken place.
May deceiving with her, or with mine
Regardless she comes or not, But the vault of My heart will be
    loaded with her affection,

8.45PM 29/11/2021

79. A Blue gown on milky way

As soon as my eyes fell on blue gown,
In which a familiar face was hidden,
When I'd look carefully,
It seemed to be overlooked,

At first I felt delusional,
Isn't this somewhere water fairy,
whose spirit is floating on blue ocean,
Splashes of whose wings bloom on my face.

When I look from afar,
The gleam of sapphire pierces my eyes,
It seems the soul of this precious stone is
Like to have descended from god,

However, if my eyes dig out the deepest Feelings into this soul,
a little milky moon appears In the blue sky, Along clouds with
black eyes

As I moved away,
It felt as if a white caterpillar was sitting on a Blue rose. Now the
conscious feels whether it Seems to be a measure of divine
power.

11.45PM 09/09/2023

80. Silent Convey love

I love a young lass, who peruses,
My words through poetry,
Her mind stays quiet,
However, she is engaged daily with my words,

While my words are dumb forever,
They can't convey by speak,
Yet, each page and sonnet demonstrate
Something about my genuine affection.

My verse book plays in her grasp,
I don't know her love intention,
Notwithstanding, I realise that her heart Never become weary of
   perusing my verse,

When I see her black eyes,
who are generally reflect
The sensations of my verse,
whose engraving is noticeable in her.

Although i haven't conveyed my love to her, But my poetry are
   adequate to Impart my True love,
Along these lines, I have explicit
My love even without expressing it to her.

8.40 PM 22/09/2021

81. I wonder! Then why are you careless?

I feel spring everywhere
when i see you
But the day you are not seen,
The world seems useless.

Feel bad for me as much as you want
But my intent is wrong with you,
Dispute as much as you want with me
But i wrote as my life is for you.

Now my say doesn't come out
Because I am fell in the grief of your love,
That's why you can listen to my heart
Through the mouth of my pen.

You're unable to count my words
But you can grasp them via my poetry.
You are a carelessly bird
As exhibited And I am a cage bird.

The fire of my love is blazing
And I am getting its warmth.
I am afraid of my love falls
Which is becoming my killer.

4.47 pm 18/07/2023

82. Why have I picked you?

My words could never explore
Since observation transcends words
The game of your sweet grinning is enduring.
Whose breakdown is to pass on from my death.

That's why I'm strolling along with your memory on love way,
My feet are following your strides
Rich aromas are floating from your way,
which never allows me to feel hunger on this street,

Which never lets me feel hunger on this road,
You have white colour symbolises purity,
Who looks like the milky rays of the moon,
The blush of your face looks so beautiful,
As if the red path of sky were thanking the setting sun,

Your black-eyes are a mirror of mine life,
That informs me of my everyday mistakes.
Your presence seems to me like this,
As revive diffuse to those sitting by the flowing fountain,

When I hold your hand I feel like,
I feel my presence next to an fairy in heaven,
whenever you call out me,
As if a goddess was calling me from heaven,

Your feet don't hesitate to move to my love-laden yard.
Like the rays of the sun towards the earth,
When I look into your eyes,
Feels as if I am reading the fable book of my love.

If I ever talk about you to anybody on the earth,
Then I only listen to the tale of your commendation
So far I have not found any malicious in you,
So I picked you Like a visually impaired person.

1.03 am 6-08-2022

83. Beauty of all angles

When my heart sits on the
Threshold of your black-eyes,
It begins to measure
Your beauty from all angles.

When it probe your beauty and
It does not see any shortcoming
Even if it is doing this work
To find out of you deficiency.

Then, not seeing any deficiency,
He would be astonish at the craftsmanship of
The one who made you,
It seems every part fitted best in its own space.

Then at the end he concludes that
God alone is such a skilled worker that
No makes an error in his own creation,
Such flawlessness can be made by his creation.

Now I say thanks to God
Who has considered me worthy
And placed me on the threshold of
His created beauty.

11.52 13/08/2022

84. A dream marriage

I dreamt that I am getting married to her,
As I gently picked her veil from her head,
her black-eyes flash my face,
As soon as I looked at her,
I was standing there with a lot of loving unspoken words.
Agony words begun to gone into my ears from around a crowd,
Maybe they having not content with our intercaste marriage,
As soon they began directing awful sentiments toward me along-
side my loved ones,
I could not bear it all and my sleep left me there,
I sat up, and saw the pearls of my tears fall down into my lap at
dawn,
I wish, if I was of the same caste, then the soul of black eyes
would be mine forever.

12.52 AM 15/08/2022

85. How could to accept

Still I want you over and over again like the shade of the forest
looks for sunny.
How would it be advisable for me to manage Your grinning black
eyes?
Obviously, the individuals who are outside sparkle.
Yet don't have inside affections for anybody
Only able to watch my laughing
But never able to mitigate my sorrow behind these.
Eyes that remain calm with my silence and
Fail to investigate the cause of my distress.
They accept my quietness as my anger
But do not see my love in my anger
Now you tell me how I can believe your black eyes.
I wish I could tell you the whole story of why
I am waiting for you on your way.

9.20 Pm 07/10/2022

86. My Even Heart Aparts Keenly

Miserably
I am on the long lasting way
That leads to endless path of love
My steps are being slowly by swelling.

Even Sadly
My feet gets tired, Even then
They are not taking the name of stopping
That are wish to stay on the destination,

Happily
I am on the perfect way,
That leads to my determine destination
It's certain to gain a fruit from my exertion.

Apathy
I am a priest of your soul
Whose black-eyes remains stay in my heart
My stubborn heart don't want to leave your track.

Keenness
My heart flowing keenly under your virtue
Who is walk along with your haughty steps
Universe verbalizes my verse love through its nature.

00.07 AM 18/01/2022

87. My Kite Of Black-eyes

Probably not here anyone,
who not get about lohri
festival of punjab in india.

known as kites fair,
A custom of all kites who
Dives into the ocean of sky.

Sky was full of kites,
My kite was fluttering on the sky,
Verified with black-eyed,

whose string is out of my hands
However,I am hunger for this kite,
My eyes are holding on to its appearance.

who is floating on the road of sky.
I am crossing many miles on field,
As pursuing this kite,

Converse about is here,
My pen write out identity,
Of black-eyes on this white kite.

please don't get on,
So, deem my endeavors,
who is looking out for this achievement.

1.30pm January (13/01/2022)

Lohri (Festival of India on whose day flying kites on sky)

88. I wish!

I can't see a single lament over the fate of Your life,

I wish!
Your pain I could write in my name,

I wish!
May the pearls of your tears be donated to me In your coming life.

I wish!
I could write the happiness of my share in Your name.

I wish!
May my heart feel the Quietness that belongs To your black eyes,

I wish!
May I fragrance so that I could share your Beauty praise across the world.

I wish!
If I were a breeze so that I could kiss The smile of your rosy lips.

I wish!
If you were in front of me, I could find my Flaws in the glass of your black eyes,

I wish!
May my soul hug your soul and sleep forever On our way of life.

I wish!
May I be busy to see the smile in your auspicious soul.

10.45PM 05/08/2022

89. A book of black-eyes

Let me compose a book,
On your sacred black eyes,
This book will impart a statement,
As a description of a love laden way.

Some of ways of your attitude is biassed
On the path of love.
While some are neutral
Thus these two are inverse to one another.

Each page has different title,
Which may be vary as per action,
Taste of these are same for everyone,
The smell of true love seems to spread from every page.

Each sonnet is streaming like a river,
Who contains many precious stones,
Every reader can plunge into such sacred stream,
The blindfold of false love can be faraway from the eyes.

Every words fragrance is endless,
Here each word turns into a companion of the eyes.
The heart wants to read over and over,
Repeatedly words make of judge true love,

17/09/2020 9.35PM

90. How to make you feel

I can see the sky and the sweltering sun,
The cool moon and the sparkling stars,
Who also behold me, but I am unable
To tell them that my heart is suffering.

I can hear the sounds of various animals and
Birds as well as I can realise their emotions,
But I cannot spell out to them
The utterance of my heart.

I can smell the flowers and Herbs
As well as the trees but
How can I make them realise
The smell of my heartache?

Similarly, I can know your emotions
From your black eyes, but
How can I make you feel the lamentation of My sorrowful heart.

12.39 pm 11/08/2022

91. Spellbound love of my heart

My heart always seeks you,
Even though my eyes search for
Your eyes everywhere
Where you don't even have black eyes.

My tirelessly eyes piercing a night
Like a firefly to find her long lasting love.
Flame of hopes are leaving from my heart,
Feelings are sailing across my heart,

The passing wind of love is teasing
My heartstrings,
The longer desire is becoming more intense,
The crooked paths of love are becoming my patience.

Waves of tune are raisin out from our hearts,
One heart is silent as if icy lake and,
Another is manifesting like waterfalls,
No corresponding of our steps is here on the love ways.

The light of dawn is breaking on my face,
That awakens my sorrowful heart,
Which brings to its yard endless torment.
which prick my heart like thorns.

Then rays of the sun come in the yard of my heart.
As much as filled my empty yard with delight,
It Keeps on fondness desire fresh
On the path of true love, To get it forever.

This is shown to us by the clouds in the sky,
As the love drops from the clouded heart on the Earth.
As the sky is never devoid of clouds
As the life of love never ends in the heart.

00.03 AM 12/08/2022

92. The turn of my love

Night has been habitual my late sleeping
My pen likewise is stirring yet to composing
A verse alongside me at 12 PM
The recollections of black eyes are lying on The bed with me
    however not resting yet.

Sun rays couldn't console me rather get Burning my love desires,
But my spirit stays drawn towards its heavenly Recognition across
    the planet.
This cycle goes on continuously

The stars also cover my eyes veil under which Conceal my sorrow
    but I am unable to dig out,
However their twinkling is a proof of
My awake late at night
They also assist me with drawing my affection line.

I think that I should leave black-eyes way and Take my love
    towards the night, sun and stars who sleep and wake up
    corresponding to mine,
Because they all are habitual in
My way of life.

23.49 pm 14/08/2022

93. Talk quietly with my eyes

I am not the owner of such personality,
That I can tell you about my love,
Because I am a lost soul in love,

Therefore I don't want to open
The door of my tongue,
You can read to my eyes to find out of my deepest love for you,

May be my eyes will let you know when you would talk them,
Please let your black eyes verbalise with eyes of mine,

I don't know how great deel I have love you, And how deep i will
    love you
But all of this is immense.

12.15AM 17/06/2021

94. Nature rejoices in the union of souls

I am thinking to explicit my love
To my black eyed darling,
Dark clouds came on yard of sky,
Along with black eyes holy spirit,
As our love proposal came.
We are swaying to declare
That the weather of rain also arrived
Along with love,
When the rain started,
We hugged tightly to each other.
When the sun came out, it saw that
We fold our arms around each other.
When the sun touched us.
We will not undoubtedly separate,
Still, we clasp hands by firmly,
Windy also came,
Who put forward our excursion,
And broughts us on top of mountains,
Where we made promises to one another
And vows not to be separated from each other
And to be together throughout our lives as well.
As soon as we came down from the mountain,
We are grateful to nature.
Who alone is the witness of our love life.

23/08/2023 2.30PM

95. I am the soil of your edges

You are the river that is streaming fastly,
You're Moving regardless of your edge,
But your banks are stable what are staring at your haughtiness,
Since i am the soil of these shore,

It's waves falling on me as a of black eyes,
In whose glance strange people are drowned,
These shores appear to be weird to you,
Your gait is flowing with pride along of their,

My soil is dissolving into your waves,
Your waves are bent on erasing my entity,
My perished is getting day by day,
And your waves have been dancing joyfully,

There will be no sound of your banks collapsing
On the day the soil of these banks will thaws
Then your conceit will be reached on peak,
You can go here and there without stopping.

The break down soil in water will go to the plains,
Your terror will increment among the people,
They will say that it didn't spare its banks,
So where will it spare us?

9.30pm 5/01/2022

96. Waking through the night of stars

Even though the night was over,
I couldn't fall asleep,
My torso is on the bed and
My eyes are fixed upwards,

Who was lost in the fair of stars
Adorable stars was reflecting frequently,
My eyes beguile with all such,
As like lover enjoys her beloved's gossip,

Did not want to leave even for a moment
Rather wished to be a piece of entirety,
Desire was to stay among them forever,
I wanted to stay in the family of these stars.

A degree was of such amuse among stars
They are compose night like the black eyes,
Whose gentle dark never pushed me to out,
Outside such dark which can cater surviving life,

Even though the day had gone up, it was not felt yet
The first rays of the sun were gone in the birds' nests
Stars disappeared in their dark, But still my eyes are open.

10.45PM 25/07/2023

97. Why don't you instead now

At the point when I will dead,
Your tears will stream down,
But, I wouldn't see Your moan,
Instead, share my suffering at now,

You will deliver blossoms
On my grave,
Whereas, I wouldn't sniff them,
So present them rather now,

You will pardon
My alleges,
But i wouldn't know so, Forget them instead now,

You will say a few words
About my commendation,
But i wouldn't hear so,
In this manner acclaim rather now,

Your black-eyes will read,
Inscribed words on my grave
But I wouldn't see so,
Thus, read my eyes's statement rather now,

You will stay some time,
Along with my grave,
But, i wouldn't feel you,
So Sit near rather now,

All your efforts will be doing to repent
In the future when i will not here,
But i wouldn't see your meaningless efforts,
But why don't you do my endorsement instead now.

17/07/2023 11.40PM

98. Statement of Black eyes's Nod

A poor lover has extreme love
For his beloved, Even if she hasn't,
Rather he immersed in his beloved love,
Regardless of whether she intends to disapprove.

At each step his endeavors goes towards her
While dearest is sloppy towards her sweetheart,
A poor lover is waiting for the movements, Which can realize his
    love to his beloved.

After many tireless exertions
Concluded that she doesn't heed,
Even though she rational at all matter
But, nonetheless not smart for true love.

Now a sweetheart arrived at in the corner,
Where found a valid reasonable matter
His beloved's eyes extremely black,
In which black clouds float often.

Who invisibles to all the sights in front,
Feasibly this reason is an hindrance,
So the messages of my love are fade away
Even altitude waves of true love unfurled.

Since it's all blame goes to the black eyes,
Although they are very charming,
However they don't perceive the worth of frontage,
Thus the sign of black clouds exhibits black darkness.

12.58am December (12/12/2019)

99. Choose your life by carefully

While you'll going out
From the darkness,
You'll call out your heart.

You will see outside
The universe,
Believing someone is hard.

Because of a false belief,
Many people will reach out to you.
However, you won't ever get to know them.

What to do on that limit,
Just a miserable wellspring
Will emerge there.

Many people you'll find here,
Who'll like you,
But not those Who will abide by you,

However, I want to warn you
To carefully look for the right lover
By looking through your black eyes.

Be kind to yourself from the bottom of your Heart at all times,
    and
Please don't be influenced by someone else's beauty wings.

If you lose heart and don't ill at ease
For genuine lover,
So I'm prepared to get by with you for the entire of my life
    sincerely.

10.15pm 10/08/2022

100. Immortal path of love

O God.., please listen my prayers,
May the days of love never be short,
For love has many things to express,
whose requires suited time to analysis,
Perhaps it's looking is even after death of lovers,

It doesn't make sense anymore,
How much time is there for someone to love,
But life seems too short to love for someone,
However, life may extend to love days.
Lend me more love for a couple of days.

Give me love for love,
Show me the way to the black eyes,
On whom I may share my love all my life
May the spring of that path also become my friend,
Then I would walk along with such spring,

It would hand out Many joys to the passers,
So my dearest won't ever be trouble in such spring,
My eyes will stroll on this way along the eyes of my dearest,
Thus the long journey of our love will long smile on this road,
Our hands will stay caught in one another's hands,

Our hearts will know one another and say I love you too,
So they will remain one another even after death,
In the next life too, they will be to be born for one another,
That's why I hope for such a path that won't allow us to be isolated
From one another all through our lives.

8.50PM 27/10/2022

101. A brilliant impressions on my heart

While your enchanting soul giggles,
It is a blessing at the forefront of my thoughts.
When your black-eyes gazed at me,
Dark mists drifting before mine,
When you sit beside me,
I view myself as a fortunately,
When you talks with me,
My emotions comes out,
When you're feet touches my feet,
Then it becomes my intention to dance with you.
When you hold my hand,
My heart wants to hug you,
When you sleeps with me,
I want the night not to be ended,
When you look at me,
My heart wants to settle down in your eyes,
When i kiss your lips,
I feels like a honey,
When your hair fall down on my face,
My sentiments of love are buried under them.

2.50pm 09/08/2022

102. Waiting for black-eyes

Love won't ever tire,
Heart never cease
Pulse keeps on,
Breath is streaming on,

I'm getting distracted,
It is becoming difficult to accost.
Steps are being slow down,
The limbs are also cooling down.

There doesn't seem to be any prospect of rehabilitation.
My hands are empty too,
There is no suffice even in the mind.
Even though eyes are tired,

This body is a stack of soil,
The weight isn't getting up from the cot,
Nobody comes to me to ask how I'm doing,
I alone am suffering all the pains.

But no one is going to share my pain,
Even rest is abhorring this pile of residue of mine,
Soul of black-eyes is not visited still,
Who will direct my soul to leave this cot.

8.30AM 05/01/2022

103. A trip to monuments

A caravan excitedly goes to a memorial,
How much they wanted to be entertained?
Mostly sunny was passing over head,
All group seemingly to be suck on fresh taste,

A gallery that we was now penetrated
For the first time,
It seems to be a dark caves like a black-eyes,
whose dark reflects in many ways informative.

Not a single corner left here who doesn't do it. Here opposite us
    Walls & statue gave
A view of whole patriotism,
Many blood feuds are displaying of country,

Still, the sight began to seem frightening
And the heart began to tremble.
As soon as we came to know about the martyrdom of our
    country,
How did we get freedom?

The lovers of the country who had such
A scene in their mind started to shed their tears,
Such a scene immediately took away
The fun of our mind & heart-wrenching.

As soon as we came out, our teacher instilled in us the love of
    patriotism,
Throughout our convictions became more
Firm towards our country,

As enthusiastically as they left,
They came back filled with grief that had Rendered them helpless,
    remembering only Their freedom heroes and nothing else.

10.19 PM 17/08/2022

104. All one indulge in love

All of us sipping tea,
All talk about the love,
Some unaware from love
Whereas some know,
Some are victim of love,
Whereas some are not,
Some say love is lied,
Some have true,
Some lover love their beloved
As she is a breath of his life.
Some express their
Unexpressed deceitful love,
Yet, how is it that i could tell that
I'm likewise casualty by black eyes,
Like the frog by snake.
Since I would rather not disprove her,
As I'm self answerable for such a wrong deal.

10.40PM 07/07/2023

105. Then be mine forever

Then why are you discussing caste?
If We are being of a similar planet,
If Our language is a uniform,
Our way of life is something alike.

Whereas our country is additionally one,
And we're creatures living under a similar roof of sky,
We need the same ingredients for living
Then why can't you be mine anyway?

Please try to spell out to your black eyes,
I want you to sit next to me,
And let your black eyes to see in my eyes,
Then let them be a couple.

Then you might be figure out my quiet love,
Then may my quiet eyes be observed,
Kindly don't converse with me about separating,
We are experiencing the same thing

We must make one soul out of two spirits
Break the bonds of these castes,
We should make one soul out of two spirits,
Break the obligations of these standings,

Put a necklace of happiness on my love's neck instead of sorrow
    rosary,
Doing this may make people angry
With you but not God.

10.25PM 10/07/2022

106. River of black eyes

I gazed couple of black cave
Which are seemed to be black eyes
Some of this is seen to be leaked
This appears to convey some secret.

As the auspicious river is streaming
Its dancing waves are cool down
The water is roaring from its banks
The mist is blurring the transparent water.

As the truth emerges from the mist,
As the valley is swept by a gentle breeze,
As everyone is asked to accept reality,
As their faces are bright with joy,

Where the mind is content with vision,
The eyes are delighted incessantly, and
All thirst is quenched,
As if kindness is being lavished.

This valuable fortune is liberated from eagerness,
As truth, kindness, genuineness and goals included,
That is all spouting on the top of water,
This is spilled out on passers-by.

Don't neglect as well as instability,
All things being equal, approach and open your hands,
Acknowledge Her beauty for future fortune,
which is a vital piece of your life,

18/12/2022 6.45 pm

107. Idol of black eyes

Whether you're a black eyes soul,
Nonetheless, you're a peace idol.

Whether you're a stir body,
However, you're a stillness idol,

Whether you're a talking,
However, you're a harmony idol.

Whether you're an onlooker,
Nonetheless, you're a spectator idol.

Whether you're a listening,
However you're an attentive idol,

Whether you're a stunning soul,
However you're a deity idol,

Whether you're a best girl,
However you're a mystically idol,

Whether you're a gorgeous,
However you're a sunny idol,

Whether you're a smart,
However you're a wisdom idol,

Whether you're an analogous,
However you're a perceptible idol,

Whether you're avoiding reflection,
However you're a black night's star idol.

9.42pm August (21/08/2021)

108. Never say again

O! Never say my heart is false,
Even in your absence, I have preserve your black eyes in mine
Although my soul can left me easily as compared to your
  recollections,

All of my flaws forced their way into my love life
Never believe in my nature rather than heart
which strives to make your desire come true
As if the heart of mine stays in the love lane.

Please don't care about my hopes
Who never back down on thee black-eyes,
That one abides by thy individual cherish, So..
Never stay away from my well-off heart.

Many fountains of pleasure are raised
Into the valley of my emotions
Where new born flowers scent out
Throughout my love, that leads to thee.

When you take breath in the wide universe,
You'll never find anyone who could devote his life. Towards your
  love except my court of heart who always seeks your lovely
  appearance.

If you would listen closely,
You will feel my pen artist to
Who is dying for thee,
As if it were dying for you. That's why my heart never stops
  beating.

12.03pm 18/08/2022

109. On the same path

Only me
And the empty road can be seen,
I am on the travel for a long time,
But no one can be seen.

I'm strolling along with my shadow,
Who stays parallel to me,
His stride is following my style of run,
Yet, l am unable to talk with him.

After numerous miles,
A squirrel saw me,
He appealed me to stay,
As well he asked me who I was looking for?

I asked about a holy spirit,
After profound thought he said,
Nobody was seen before you,
Except for a blonde young lady with black eyes.

Thanks oh god to grace,
My steps are not squandering on my path,
One day will certainly come to meet us both,
I'm fortunate that I am likewise in a similar way.

Now my shadow started
Walking quicker than me.
And I also started following him,
So that the day of meeting black eyes can come soon.

13/06/2022 10.45 PM

110. Invisible promise

She said, l am sorry for your choice
She said, I am sad for your hollow heart
She said, l am on the wretched way for your love
She said, I am on an endless path regardless of you.

She said we'll never met in this birth,
She said we'll complete our love in the next life.
She said we'll be reunited again,
She said we'll be met in threshold of heaven,

How can l feel your such commitment,
Which imparting from every words,
But Give me a love letter stamped with your black eyes, then I
    will reconcile that letter with your commitment.

9.45Pm 27/09/2022

111. Distance never matter on the road of love

It's never matter the amount you're far away,
But you always live in my heart,
It doesn't make any difference to me that you don't converse with
me,

I realise that your black eyes disregarding me, nothing matter,
But I don't know why I'm still insane behind these,
In any case, I'm not having an opportunity to say I love you.

Your illiterate black eyes are unable to recognize the love in my
eyes,
And your youth has bent on my heart's desires.
My sentiments are brooking under your pride,

What can I do? Despite your hypocrisy,
I can still do this: I will always love you, Remember you, treat you
with respect, and Ask the universe to look after you forever.

I have established a routine even in the absence of you.
As I still love you.
Hate doesn't matter how much I love you,

1.00AM 06/01/2023

112. Jolt of love life

Just
I'm a suffering soul,
I have some thinking,
I'm living soul,

About
I'm on the way
That is deal with me
Like a nonliving things,

Seemingly
A worthiness is paying
To my falling perspiration,
A warm pampering is consuming my life,

Mostly
Not A little bit love on my way as well,
Except hate,
That Pierce me inside reliably consistently,

Internally
My breath feeling on the way as counting,
As it is going to stop
Should be inquired,

Never
I followed the way as love ,
But I have never felt that
It goes to black-eyes,

Don't
A little tear couldn't fall down too,
But all feelings are inhumed under
The glare of thundering eyes.

Ever
Whenever you think,
You will be familiar with my closeness,
You will have voyaged a great deal in your life.

Reality
Then, despite your efforts,
The distance between us will never be less,
You will be left with tears.

8.40pm 12/07/2023

113. When I am with you

When i am with you
I feel happiest then,

My mind never stay
Anywhere except your thought,

My heart beats effortlessly
In close proximity to your soul.

Reading your black-eyes statement never
Made my eyes tired,

Listening to your sweet voice never made
My ears tired,

Playing with your hands never made
My hands tired,

My feeling to seduce you
Which peruses to your attitude,

Sparkling of your face
Rinses my sluggishness,

My nose keeping on sniff
Your Heart's blossoms of affection,

My saplings of affection are developing
In the nursery of your heart's yard, maybe.

17/08/2021 12.19PM

114. Please come to my heart's Home

Where did the black eyes go?
Who are the reflection of my life path
Touch of whose rays drive my heartbeat, And
Who wanders aimlessly like the wind?
Please come to the home of my heart.

If I knew where you were,
I would beg you to come to
My heart's home by holding your arm.
But I don't know where you are.
Please visit my heart's place.

It has been waiting ever since the morning, Like the rain of a
    drought,
Morning has turned into evening and
Night has fallen & darkness turned to black
Kindly Come to the home of my heart.

I call for the moon and the stars,
I asked from the trees of forest too,
And asked from all the birds,
No sleep is taking place to my eyes,
no where
Kindly come to the home of my heart.

Oh God, please find her and bring her to me
Tell her the depressed mood of my heart,
Say with your own grace,
His soul is slipping away without you
Please return to my hear.

8.30 pm 23/05/2023

115. Please don't look as....

Kindly don't ask my caste,
Don't gaze like that at me? I am human too
Why do you see my black colour?
But look at my sunny toil too
Don't think about my useless face
But check my capacity out also
Don't look at my lonely poverty,
Check my generous heart too
Please don't look into my sad eyes,
But see my bliss in your own black eyes,
Don't look at my torn shoes,
But look at my miles journey on foot,
Please don't see at my greyish hair,
But look also at my life experience,
Please don't look at my credentials
But forget not to see my wisdom,
Please don't keep on remember my name,
But keep on remember my given help you in necessity,

27/12/2022

116. Elixir of life

Your heart has not yet tasted love
Whenever you do, you will feel the suffering of love,
Whether you do it with your spouse
Or with your child.

The smell of the plant of love goes far
Which you can smell in your relatives and local area as well
You will likewise see some of them eating the fruit of the affection
   tree
As the guardians of their child in the oldest age.

You can't smell it however you can definitely see the love of
   Mother Earth
Who nurtures her children with a lot of pampering love
Which feeds them when they need it.
Furthermore, fills the laps of her kids with gifts.

Then your bosom will be loaded up with love
You will likewise spread love around you then
People will come forward to take your affection
Yet, I will stand far away because I recognize your black eye's love.

11.30 PM 08/01/2024

117. Xenium of Basant

Yellow yellow eyes seeing
Golden rays are piercing
My heart is being annoying.

Yellow yellow flowers rise
Carry on waving also sans bias
The Breeze is a strolling mass.

Yellow yellow sun rise
Fall on the snow rise
See on the cold rush.

Yellow yellow a butterfly
Flee about to Happy shy
Dive on the garden fly.

Yellow yellow think again
Black eyes doing bargain
Never ever gain by a clever brain.

Yellow yellow fire is flowing
Flames is jumping cool down
Hunger mingles with the moans.

Yellow yellow spring came
Shade of felicity is playing a game
Verdure is getting up once again.

Yellow yellow are my sore
Your like cat's eyes explore
My lost energy yellow sunny restores.

3.15 PM 12/10/2023

Seasons (Basant)

118. Please don't do more

I don't know,
How many hearts robbed,
How many hearts will be robbed,
Why don't you explain your black-eyes ?

A few people are buried.
Additionally, many will be more,
Did you never hear them crying? Nonetheless, their gravestones
   show that they were silent.

Even though some victim,
My heart also victim by your black-eyes
So my existence will be no more,
However, these are not satisfied.

Sharp arrows are left fastly by these,
Your eyes has injured many lovers,
Some hearts have stopped beating,
And many are counting the last beats,

Some people fall themselves in this pool,
They would sunk,
Some will be attractive to its banks,
And some wish to dip in this river.

Please don't do so murderous,
Otherwise, you will not get salvation
in your next life either.
So, do what is valid to your life.

Your black eyes also earn fury,
who prey on people every day,
Your tears don't even flow,

But if you go through their graves,
you will definitely get a sense of life and death.

10.45 PM 31/07/2022

119. Recollections of black eyes

Numerous recollections are here,
Who are liquefying like glacial masses,
Which are currently streaming like a waterway,
Through which my cerebrum and heart are streaming.

Nobody is attempting to draw out,
All disclosure pours on water And floating hastily by disperse,
Many are perusing disclosure words.

The Black Sea, which is looking for such memories,
Appears to be the destination of the flow of memories.
As soon as these memories fall into the Sea, Her black eyes
   awaken from sleep.

All recollections are blended
Into black-eyes of the ocean.
Since it's recollections of black eyes
Who set up memories here and finished as well.

10.45pm 14/06/2023

120. Fulfil my love

My love for you grows deeper every day,
My mind is enjoying the essence of my love.

Everywhere, you memory are the most sweetest.,
Your beauty is like a gentle white rose.

Happy grin of your face is just about as sweet as honey,
The blush of your cheeks resembles the delicate petals of a rose,

As your black eyes shimmer like night stars.
Your character is so noteworthy and glorified.

Know my affection to previously and investigate new matter,
America has been your favourite for a long time.

So my pen has been writing around for you since long ago.
But your poetry book about black eyes is all set to take you to the
    United States.

During our journey,
People will gather to admire your beauty in a sprinkle,
Just like they do in India to see a goddess.

Despite the fact that we were together in front of each other in
    college,
But my quiet love remained mute.

Even though my love for you only lasted five months,
Nevertheless it will never change And it will never end.

My love for you is unlike any other,
But your poetry book of black eyes will preserve your grace and
    beauty forever.

11.45AM 19/01/2022

121. Looking for black eyes ways

My 31 Dec night passed away
With dark black night,
My eyes wait up another
Black eyes Indication,
My eyes set up on way of
New night, but blanked.
My eyes keep on invigorated
On a foggy darkest night.
My eyes look on deserted night
Long way of black eyes.
My eyes asked the dark way
But ignored by the mysterious night.
My eyes feel out heart beat
Of the darkest night's pace.
My eyes look for whole night
The way of black eyes.
My eyes a proof of dark night
What is going on into the dawn.
My eyes recollect of previous
Endure 31.12.2019 first meet.
My eyes pleased to recollection
2020 new year phone chat.
My eyes still open while day
Came to duty, night faded.
My eyes would remain opened
Ever to come to black eyes.

1.45AM 31/12/2020

122. Black eyes in the yard of nature

Torso of mine yet steeped in deep sleep,
While my eyes are open by obscure,
Slanting light playing with early dawn,
Black clouds compete with racing
On the road of sky with a thunder voice.
Breezes are jumping upon the black clouds.

Various birds divers into the valley of
Black clouds who are kidding with nature,
They singing hymns to the commendation of nature,
To whose lap they are getting warmth like mother earth.
Seemed to be a peaceful ocean at sunrise.

Trees also a proof of quivering
Who also dancing with swaying all around
They are also singing sweetly,
They are showering leaves on earth.

Drizzling welcomed caused by earth,
My soul drenched with nature blessing,
While my vision fell on the black clouds.

No one was want to leave such a happy yard
I was also absorbed in the black eyes along with nature.

So, I was creating my poem to such a loving nature.

                                    10.15pm July 23/07/2019

123. Rather True love is an opportunity

Perhaps you don't know
About the true love,
But you can deem it
When you will see my eyes,

True love is that which
Ask nothing,
Rather which remains
Silent to an extent.

So i am not asking you
Anything
But i am waiting your side love,
Because Time is eternal for my love,

So, Don't let overlooked
My true love by your black-eyes,
Rather investigate the way
Of my true love.

True love never be ended,
It will never be died,
Rather it will survive after death,
Thus my True love is an opportunity for your life.

6:10pm 19/07/2023

124. Glimpse of heaven's beauty

What a lucky day it was
When the deity of beauty sat close to me,
But this luck was seemed short-lived,
I wish to God that I get more time,
Yet, it was not in his will,

My mind was craving to time,
Because time nodding me not to remain more,
But my heart was full fleshed of Merry
As nothing was going on.
Even though I was talking with the beauty of a deity,

Golden beams of Even the sun paled before her beauty,
When I'm unable to meet his milky gentle face,
But her bright black-eyes are gesturing to me to stay more.
But time was holding my arm and lifting me up,
Now I didn't know whether to acknowledge the time or her
black-eyes.

11.30PM 12/05/2022

125. Be careful on the commendation of love

Damn! thirsty darlings & thirsty lovers,
If you came out for the journey on the love way,
Listen to my song carefully then that you haven't ever listen,

My love journey was much longer in previous eras, but it is now
   too long.
Whose conclusion has not yet arrived.
My excursion alongside my life prompts a pathless way.

On the love roads, numerous lovers and loved ones appear.
All vacant hands are gesturing that affection having nothing,
Many people are carrying on with tears in their eyes.

Some was robbed by black eyes and others with cat eyes,
But only the chuckle of love was spilling into the way,
Nothing else beside it.

Many people nodding to others for not taking on this road,
Numerous pangs of distress are Carried on their heads.
That appears to wheeze at them.

Here the situation is now same for all
Love having nothing except deception,
Where love first feels for then made friends Afterwards, robbed
   by it and slayer prop sympathy.

Come on through the yesteryear ways or new,
There is a need to remain with understanding,
Although might be a confluence of sorrow or happiness,
Yet your will might betray you on love commendation.

                                          00.37AM 24/08/2022

126. My unstoppable path

I would like to expend my life with thy, and
I know, you don't have love for me
But I having a lots of love for thy,
Please don't open the gates of thy tongue.

Be that as it may, continuously keeping
The entryways of thy black eyes open,
With whom I'm busy talking quietly.
Whose silence quenches my thirst for love.

O my love, you are the never-ending way of My destination.
I am walking with the intention of conquering It.

I will keep on following this way peacefully,
I will quietly walk on this silence path entire my life,
You just need to welcome my calm steps on Your tender soil.

If the dust of your route makes me so dirty that My existence
should not be seen by anyone on the road,
So that the passers-by do not recognize me,
I will always be grateful to you.

Thus, as long as the doors of your black eyes are open to me,
I will continue on this path, until the day
These doors are closed to me
And my life will end there and fall down.

9.45PM 14/05/2020

127. Nightmare

A night was a cruel,
I fell asleep early,
I dreamt,
Which bothered me a great deal.

I saw a second shoreline of river,
On which I saw
A beautiful lass with a black eyes,
Whose didn't be mindful of me,

While I am calling out her,
She was meandering all over
As if she was doing some probe,
She is basking in her fun,

She is go to stroll forward,
I also began following her without a moment's delay,
I started drowning in the water of the river,
I woke up as soon as my head went under the water,

Now I'm feeling that reality will be something very similar,
I realised if my destination is
She the one I'm chasing,
And Then why it's drowning me.

4.37 pm 11/08/2022

128. A journey with the queen of fairies

What a beautiful journey,
When a lover along with Brownie,
Where two hearts be seated,
Even if they was remain silent,

But waves of hearts are crashed on the love road,
Their emotions dispersed,
As soon as one heart comes forward to say something,
And the other heart retreats,

Still, both hearts seem thrilled,
In addition two black-eyes also come into sight,
Who peer at them,
They are also demure to say anything,

Yet from the left heart was pouring a flood of love,
whom against those black eyes couldn't stand,
But they were slipping in such a flow of love,
This trip seems too short.

But the loving heart wants to carry on,
An endless journey with that black-eyed fairy.
Thus such journey must be endless,
In this way, two hearts will travel through life as each other's
     escort.

00.23 Am 15-07-2023

129. My Love will always be in your love

I love you very much
Like you hate me.
As much as you used to hate me
I loved you more and more.
As much as you will hate me
I will love you more.
You just keep doing your duty
And I'm playing mine.
You are doing this freely by your own accord,
And I am doing it willingly too.
You may be stubbornly thinking this.
That many people are crazy
On your seemliness.
But that won't happen forever.
Because this form will not last forever.
While I will love you forever.
But my mind is doing all this without thinking.
But I have loved you so much
And still do and will do more.
But one day your dark eyes will yearn,
For the faithfulness of my love.
Like hot desert sand for rain.
But that time will have passed
Then like the shadow of the sun.

11.45pm 17/09/2023

130. I want you to be the gardener

I wish you were gardener
In the park of my heart,
Where the trees of my sentiments are long, These trees are getting
    bald and drying up.
You could watch the falling leaves.

You can even smell
Its pleasant blossoms,
They are now shrivelling
And their fragrance falling off.
Now leaving only their thorns.

You can likewise feel
The sounds of the birds of this garden.
Which are slowly vanishing,
Now who will build nests
On the trees of this garden?

Glory of this garden is fading away
In this way you can see
Along with this garden
Its owner is also drying up,
Nothing is going well.

I want you to become its gardener
So that the lives of many species can be saved in this garden.
So If your black-eyes supervision this garden, Then, like before,
There will be hustle & bustle in all creatures,

11.13 13/08/2022

131. Why are you for me on earth?

If you need to ask me, for what reason are you for me? You must
   know
When my sentiments locked in your black eyes,
Then the world has vanished ahead me,
I'm trapped in intricacy, what to do next ?
Seems like a pours colossal rainfall rush on the way, and storm
   blocked a road by pushed,
Where my sentiments and inclination forestall for a little while,
While I couldn't ever explore my assertion.

Until I see you,
The epic sun in my heart's yard doesn't sparkle, and the moon and
   powers of fate don't arise arranging in perfect order.
While you're playing with Your versatile as well as resting,
Then, my sentiments are being discouraged by your staggering
   dissimulation
That is the reason behind this shroud, Whereas you are living
   solace,

you'll perceived all this,
when you'd walk along me on the road of life,
when the world seems you're also too right, true and fair,
People'll commend your black-eyes recognition,
You'll feel cheerful yourself in the hands of Mother Earth, who
   pampers you,
Now you will understand well why you are on the earth for me?
Then, the people will play with my affection for them.

12.20pm 30-07-2022

137

132. Don't pass up this love door

Never think you'll come again,
Nobody can overcome death,
Let me open my whole heart,
Don't let me hide anything from you.
This life doesn't come back over and over.

Don't consider it you own,
Nothing here is yours,
Everything has been taken from here,
Everything will remain here,
This life doesn't come back over and over.

Only virtue of love will hold on,
Whose blanket will never be toren,
Warmth will be in whose chest.
Every soul would like to swing on this hammock.
This life doesn't come back over and over.

My affection will diffuse joy on your way,
There will be rapture in your smoothly ways,
So don't pass up on this open door of love,
Therefore, take love and offer love,
This life doesn't return back over and over.

8.35PM 21/06/2022

133. Strangers

Am I unusual? Am I a stranger?
Are you aware? Are you aware?
However, I don't have any idea,
For what reason am I still a stranger?
Whereas my character is like the human being,

I know all faces, and
So does my soul by them, Here,
Only a silence is known as a sign of respect,
And a small nod suffices.

A life identity has death at the end,
No one has an identity,
No matter how many souls live here,
But nobody wants to hang out with anyone,
So the values don't stay the same.

Most black-eye dwellers live here,
Whose eyes clouded with pride & arrogance.
One who doesn't feel better in trustworthiness and goodness,
Continues to plunge into the expanse of their haughtiness,
Because of this they do not seem to have any of their own but all
    unfamiliar blood,

Now I can judgement,
I belonged to that city,
where clouds of arrogance and glory hover,
The revenge has made me wet too,
That's why people treat each other strangers,

1.17am June (13/06/2022)

134. Suffering of poors

Poverty is nothing less than a curse,
Lakhs hardships here,
Thousands confusion here,
Limitless torment here,
Birth pushes out to be lifeless,
Death eats inside by surviving,
Pains and suffering are here,
Have to endure alone,
Friends also not make without rich,
No one also falls in love with poor,
Poor are a mocking character
No one sympathises with him,
If their hard work flows a success,
Then people start hating him.
No one listen them,
All one bothers them,
However they persevere through all the torment,
Because they are struggling
With the issue of livelihood,
There is anyone whose
Tears can reflect a pity.
It seems no community lives here,
Who can engage in the service
Of human beings without meaning,
As Black-eyes souls living here
Who doesn't see anyone do well except selfish.

12/04/2021 11.45PM

135. Why're you always

When passing a day without you,
It's appears to be a long span,
When I'm alone with you on day,
It's appears to be extremely short.

When I read a little page,
I exhaust straight away,
But i never weary when
I study your black eyes statement,

When i wait for someone person
I get tired very quickly,
But why am I not exhausted?
When I wait for you, as i still await

I quickly get tired of listening
To anyone's words,
But I never become weary of conversing
With you, I don't know why.

I soon forget all thoughts and things,
But your thoughts stay
In my mind forever,
And they never forget.

5.40 pm 10/08/2022

136. God will not let injustice

My eyes fell on the cheerful air,
As if I had just awoken.
The sun was just beginning his journey,
And every green leaf was moving on the trees.

Mist is rambling aimlessly across the environment,
Every one of the birds are shuddering,
However they are chirping by peeping,
The earth is moving in its merry way.

Recollections are showering upon me like raining down,
But these are not aligned with past,
Rather are for what's in future,
It appears to be a warmth for a blissful soul.

I long for her to be here with me,
I want to take care of her, and
I want to give her a warm hug in such a bitter cold
So that the love I have for her will warm her.

I wish I could see her sadness in her black eyes;
Perhaps it stems from her poverty;
However, the sunshine of my love will extinguish such poverty.
Then, Her yard will experience waves of happiness and
    prosperity.

Maybe her every pleasure be deliver
Might she outlive with no regrets,
But my remorse will never be outlast,
But beseech of me is to God.
Who establishes a human duo on this earth.

Society is evicting me but I complain
That my beloved is also in the same queue.
Only here the supreme justice, God'

Who could brave my nervous back soul.

I now have faith in my God
Who will not let injustice happen to me. And Will judge my right
  in making my love perfect. And I am entitled to a perfect love.

12.10AM 27/03/2021

137. Delusion of auspicious soul

If i see a swarm of black clouds,
Appears as though your dark hair is waving,

Whenever i see stars at night
Seems as though your black eyes is shimmering,

If i see a leaves of white rose,
Seems as though a dimple is turning on your cheeks.

When I see a bunch of fairies,
I attempt to looking for you among them,

When i sniff a scent on mountain,
Your existing is realised me frequently, but don't know why

If I hear the sound of the gentle wind
Your voice Begins ringing in my ears,

Whenever I see white pearls,
I get an illusion of your smiling teeth.

If i see a gait of peacock,
The illusion of your walking falls.

Whenever i see you real,
I get confused about the form of the goddess,

8.45PM 18/09/2022

138. Surviving under the dark of black-eyes

You gone away like water of streaming river,
Like thirsty tree but i am stayed yet,
I stand by your concern,
Who is getting dry gradually.

As if centuries had passed,
No a little reflection exposed,
But long lasting hope to view it
As love laden way also being shrinking,

No one seems to be coming back,
The way of detachment is becomes longer,
Whose distances of tracks are measureless,
Just a barren yard contains a forest of dreams.

But i can die,
Like a drying tree who is dying,
As the clouds are not given a letter but still have to wait for the
    rain.

07.15AM 18/12/2021

139. Your tricks on the love way

You love your black dress,
But you hate my black colour,
You afraid from black clouds,
But your eyes are black,
You travelled with strange persons,
But you afraid beside me,
Your smile spread among strangers
But your silence avoid my sight always,
I don't understand your love tricks
Even if you hide every lover
In the bosom of your shape,
But no one reaches
In the courtyard of your heart.
What to do with the beautiful face
If your heart is not clean
Why strangers don't consider
About your lying tricks on the way they love?

12.30 AM 19/09/2023

140. I Settle Down My Poem

By my will,
I chose you
Not coincidentally,
Nor, fortunately,
Because of my hard work,
Thus got a kind of fruit,
First I read your black eyes,
Not only I did read, But also observe,
Then I write about them,
Not only explored but also analysis.

I also count your influence,
Not just mention of you,
I absorb the rays of your black eyes,
Then I know nothing in the dark,
When I smell your heartbeat,
Then feels your emotion,
Then I wrote the statement of your eyes,
which display innumerable inscriptions,
I measure your steps on the path of love,
Then I change my writing accordingly.

I love dimple on your cheeks,
Then I kiss on these,
When I think about your seemliness,
Then I settle down my poem,
When I see a smiling on your lips,
Then my heart smiles but my lips not,
When I see a blinking your black-eyes,
Then many changes comes to a write poem.

10.45PM 17/10/2023

147

141. Punishment is its suffering

Alone a black-eyes soul lived at a haunted home, Around which
there was forest.
Whose window and doors Had got termites, Around which there
was no other house,
Only wind penetrated in it,

Nobody was resident
Except suffering soul Whose identity was at Uninhabited home,
Even though she was serving a sentence in it, She was happily
here.

Her curly tresses hide her black-eyes
And the rest are falling on her back and breast,
And she sat with the support of a broken cot.
Now her weak lass sat on earth counting her Event distress with
her fingers.

As robbed this home by it's Happiness and pleasure,
No worthy stock was lying Except dirty walls, The roof was also
raking soil on her head,
It looked like a house from
A bygone era tradition.

It seemed as if the one who destroyed
The house was suffering the punishment for What he had done,
Whose times had come.
Every man has days as per his actions in life.

Now find out if whether someone's happiness was robbed
And someone got sorrow,
Those who took away their happiness were Giving bad luck to
that soul,
Now this soul seemed to be a witch who was paying her dues,

5.05pm 18/08/2022

142. Sting of black eyes

Like a black snake sting,
Whose poison is rising,
My limbs being numb,
Whose pain is increasing,

Kindly take me to physician,
Who may consider my suffering.
He would check my stinging,
Who could arrive at my pain location.

No indication of stinging found,
Although no effort was spared,
Lips and mouth turned into black,
Becoming more difficult to survive,

No effect was here after exertion,
My body blacking with steadily,
Not a stinging by black snake, said mockingly, Instead, it seems,
    the black eyes stung.

12/05/2022 11.05 pm

143. Let your shadow grasp my love

Who should I explain?
I don't even have any friends.
To whom I can tell about my love,
But I want to make my wish reach you.

But I have never seen any friend even with you, Except your
    shadow,
Now sometimes I think,
Desire to sit under your Shadow's shade.

So that my peace can express love to your shadow,
It would perhaps understand my love vehemence,
Because I have no other option
To let my love reach you.

When your shadow enjoys the heat of my love,
It will be warm along with rays of your black-eyes.
These will understand the passion of my love
That burns within me.

Please don't prevent me,
And let me sit under your shadow,
Let me disclose to you my love.
I am not your enemy but your lover.

4.50 pm 27/07/2023

144. Zest of Love looks like..

Love looks like summer
Which is kissed every day
By the sun's beams
It keeps getting hotter every day
No one can escape its warm rays.

Where the cold wave moves
Where many living things are numb
And deprived of their work,
Where the cold sand keeps sliding
Love looks there like a moon.

Love looks like a night,
Where dark falls around it,
When a black-eyes soul meet
Their darkest magic is expanded then,
Which is able to cheat blindly to any person.

Love looks like a greenery
Where all forest and the garden
Remain green forever
Even though its energy is gone
But these stand with surviving hopes.

Love looks like a universe,
If someone enter in this courtyard
Who forgets himself and wanders freely.
Who remains absorbing its hustle & bustle,
Where love is seen everywhere.

4.40 pm 12/08/2022

145. Dying Ocean

Nothing is immortal,
No day stays forever,
Even though by come in turn,
Every moment will be lost,

Every night has in guest position,
Even light can't remain scattered,
No sun remains blossom,
All rays of moon will be hide,

All vegetation will dying,
Poor birds also a guest for some days,
No animals are grazing on next days,
Life of insects will be cease till the end of the day,

No tree remains evergreen,
Flows of air is switching all the time,
Glaciers disappearing even though rehabbing,
No season wouldn't be stayed on the years,

So i remind you that all things
Will be flowing into the dying ocean,
Your black-eyes will also closed by perpetual,
Ash of Your gorgeous body will dispel through the blaze.

If it's my turn today,
Then it's your turn tomorrow
So leave your pride and hold my hand
And we live happily for four days in this life.

11.45.pm may (11/05/2022)

146. Vent in your pride

Nothing have you,
Then why do arrogance,
Even if you have a lot of faith,
However, that is all you have from others,

You are not like such here,
You here lying by you're excellence
Birth have also given you by others
Why Not your endeavours for the rest of the world then.

Even your emblem is not your
Which is sprinkled by the others mouth,
It granted by your parents or relatives,
Rather it is conceded by themselves.

You here with your pride as you deemed, Your intelligence that
    conveyed through,
Your genuine schooling which is imparted you,
You're your teachers. thus it is not yours rather by others.

Your underhanded charming gave the feeling that
Others were being hoodwinked,
But it was pointless to appear such a gift of heavenly
    masterfulness.
So it's not your creation.

Even though you're black-eyes Grace
Reflection as per the willingness of nature
Which create of delusion before all one,
As black clouds that are also created by God.

3.15pm June (21/06/2022)

153

147. My drawbacks

Please.....
Is there anyone here ?
Who make of my faults,
Whether I am degree holder,
However, I am unable access to faults,
Please..... call in,

Please....
Pay to taunt me,
Rather, I knew error of mine,
Even if, No one has perfection,
Please.... carry out,

Please.....
Revealing mine,
That, draw out my flounder,
Don't need me inter into like others,
Please.... search in,

Please....
Don't hesitate
Reflecting my deficiency,
Whereas, every one deal with,
Please..... try it,

Please....
See over my hidden faults,
Let not allows me concealing faults,
Whether, everybody interesting to conceal,
Please.... lay down

Please.....
Let me allow to explain away,
If, No take me on, through mine research,

Perhaps, I black, dwarf, weak, ignorant,unknown,poor
Please.... sure it,

Please....
Don't make a guile,
Alone dig out my drawbacks,
But these by nature not mine mistake, Please.... consider it,

Please.....
Call down to nature,
Born pleasance people,
Who free from such drawbacks, Please... call down,

Please.....
Recognise the truth,
Perhaps, due my these drawbacks,
I am still a one sided lover and celibacy, Please.... justice it.

Please.....
There is anyone here?
Who can act as a mediator
Between me and the black eyes
Please.....do it must

Time:-   12:15 am
Date :-   04:06:2020

148. Heart and eye's conversation

Heart frequently remarked,
"You tricked me."

Anyway it's my daily duty,
To enter something, said eyes.

But, however also duty to
Probe into anyone, Heart said.

But, I could check it out externally,
Can't do it internally, said eyes,

But you mustn't allow the black eyes to enter
Who came along black clouds. Heart said,

But I am unable to recognize colors,
They came with silent of mind, eyes said,

How can you prove it, that
Black eyes were stillness idols, Heart said.

Rather, her white color seems prosperity mass
Who exploring light within the darkest, eyes said,

I think they resemble your friends,
To whom you did not inquire, Heart said,

But, now they reside on your backyard
So you should decide not to keep them, eyes said

But now they have become my permanent residents
So it is difficult to uproot them now, Heart said

We agreed with our mistakes,
Who ruled on you illegally by darkness. eyes said.

But, these black clouds desire to disperse
Night across the world, Heart said.

Nonetheless, we would guide them,
When we will meet them on our paths, Eyes said.

Please.... do such tell them, that
The existence of heart broken as smothered by their residing,
  Heart said.

Sure... let me met her eyes to support,
So I will clarify the worth of the heart to them, Eyes Said.

Each unfortunate heart has to ingest such eyes for genuine
  romance
That can plant the blossoms of love. Heart said

You write a letter of yours to me,
I will ask them to read this letter. Eyes said.

Here my letter proves that your darkness has extinguished
My light due to which my life is dying. Heart Said.

While I asked them to read it,
They tore the letter and did not read it. Eyes Said.

The heart once again said to the eyes that
It is all your fault for sheltering the black eyes. Heart Said.

Eyes said, it takes two to make a raw,
Not the only one me, rather we both are together.

10:49 pm June (29/06/2021)

149. I hope your condolences

I wish l could see you once more & once more
Along with me on the threshold of love,
But time wouldn't allow you same,
I can consider the pre planned time.

My heart feels your suffering,
Who doesn't want to see your tears
My eyes keep reserves your black eyes memory,
Who inscribe on my eyes by silently,

If possible, pray to God,
For me, so i can bravely bear
The sorrows of my heart on love way,
l hope you must followed my said,

I am always ready to give you happiness.
That would give you solace life,
My attempting will never end for you,
You can examine it anytime.

You must be condolences
To helping others lifeway,
We must provide solace
So that lives can be preserve more & more forever,

14/08/2021 12.10AM

150. How hard is it to keep loving?

Everyone knows the love way
They considered it easy to love,
But anyone never know
How hard is it to keep loving?

So i am doing still,
Although I am getting old,
In my love
My age doesn't hold any obstacles.

But to me my beloved's black eyes
Look like dark night,
Which is a wall between us,
In My love and her thinking,

Such a dark night prevents her
To see my love exertion and
My love also failure to realise her
As My soul lent towards her soul.

Such a dark night prevents her
To see my love exertion and
My love also failure to realise her
As My soul is groping towards her soul.

Now let a shining sun come
Among us to dispel
This gross darkness with its flames.
So that we can know each other behind the disguise.

10.45 PM 12/09/2023

151. Don't Break My Heart

Even if you break everything
Who man made,
It doesn't matter.

But don't break my heart
what is made by God,
Because it will feel sinful to you.

But my heart is alive,
Don't break it,
Have mercy on it.

They will not have any pain,
Whatever soulless around you
Even if you erase their existence.

But it is my heart
That a soulful is
Please don't ache it.

Please open the doors of
Your black eyes
And let my heart dwell there.

My heart will pray for prosperous life
In the courtyard of your black eyes,
Where your soul will dwell with a blissful life.

11.05 pm 20/07/2023

152. Mirror of black-eyes

I see a mirror again & again,
Into your black-eyes,

Nothing found here
Except black clouds,

My heart is also shaking with fear
From the roaring sound of the black clouds.

The courtyard of our love is visible with
The light of the shining sky

Rain going to come down
But yet not fall on,

The thick darkness of
The black clouds are hiding my cat-like eyes.

The impression of affection isn't noticeable
In this mirror,

However, downpour of affection can be Anticipated from such
clouds,

When I will get wet
Under this downpour,

Whose briskness will stir
The resting feelings of love in my chest.

9.20PM 15/06/2023

153. Life of a beauty after death

The legitimacy of your magnificence isn't for eternity,
However, the legitimacy of my uprightness is until the end of
    time,
So don't be glad for your excellence,
As I'm not glad for my prudence.

Your beauty resembles the leaves of a tree,
Which will one day dry up,
But, maybe my way of behaving resembles the shade of a banyan
    tree,
Whose shade will always remember the person who sits under it,

Indeed, even these delicate cheeks of yours,
One day will shrivel like roses,
Even these delightful bruised black eyes of yours,
One day they will close like lotus blossoms in dry mud,

Your life will also be panting to death,
Like an arid camel of desert.
Then your beauty will be overlooked,
Nobody will think often about your life then.

Where will your grinning & thrilled beauty go?
Nobody here knows
Then your breath will run out,
Like the comely butterfly of the desert,

After that, the wind and rain will arrive,
Which will burried your beauty by its muck,
Following a few days your beauty will likewise die.
Then people will forget your beauty too.

3.30 pm 15/07/2023

154. Talk then becomes, If you do

My composition of black eyes poetry book is of no use unless you don't read it

I love however much I can, I do more than also, but there is no use until you realise it.

However much I think about you, there is no use, until you don't understand.

I'm quiet however my quiet is of no use until you don't talk.

If I am helpless, what then, but you are not.

If I am the spring of the desert, then you are the spring of ever-green. If you want, make me the spring too.

If my life is colourless, you can fill my liveliness with colour.

There is no use in looking at you until you stop overlooking me.

If I am negative, then you are positive, make me positive too.

If I am the path, What then, then you become its track,

If I am life then you be its breath to keep it alive,

11.25 Am 28/07/2023

155. Request to nature

Nature came, Nature came,
Nature brought with the wind

Breezing brought comfort with her
Comfort brought sleep with her

Sleep brought dream with her
Dream brought Fairy with her

Fairies come with their black eyes
Black eyes brought joy with her

Joy brought with it dark clouds
Black clouds rained a lot

In which my sleep was flow
From which I woke up

Waking didn't find my value
My time lost mine too,

Nothing came to hand,
I wish to nature to come back again today

Bring black eyes girl with her
Match me with black eyes forever

And quench my thirst for life
I will be Thankful to you

I will be your obedient forever.
My journey of love will also end

12.15 PM 21/05/2019

156. Let's be a husband and wife

Let's be a husband & wife,
Trying to know each other needs,
Don't make a difference
We must not show off,

We need for Felicity,
Red blood is donating us a love life,
Oxygen lets us breathe
Cool water is also expressing our love.

Let's play in a lap of nature,
Nature contains human, animals, birds
And trees who all are our whole love lovable,
We can't stay cheerful without the hustle of the earth.

Let's give help to others,
Don't break aspirations of surviving,
Listen always shout of mother earth,
Which stays survive us look after.

Never give a pain your mother,
Whose lap warmth always reach your golden eyes,
Don't neglect the virtue of your mother,
Who never bias among its offspring.

Let's be a spouse
We all equal offspring of mother earth,
Try not to disregard submit to your mom earth,
Let us generally to be in Her will as spouse and wife.

By open your black eyes accept her grace
Along with my hands.
We will survive without hurdles
But along with the interference of nature will.

12.30 PM 02/01/2024

157. I never conveyed her my love

Our exertion are going on waste,
Although we are staying
On the front of one another
Many times in the love way.

My cat-like eyes and his black eyes
Often talk silently while they meet incidentally. But in their
   glance,
Many love affairs are hidden,

I had never chance to say I love you
And i miss you too,
The mountain of my longing
Stays standing like dry reeds.

Yet, I have intense desire to convey,
I love you a great deal,
I know my ambition are worthless until
She is ready to listen my love words,

However even my purposeless endeavours Keeps remain rather
   new
To arriving in my adored's heart,
My eyes are in waiting for her love meeting,

No day is passed aside from your recollect,
Regardless of how far you from me
You live in the office of my heart,
You just need to talk to me wherever you're.

Once more, As long as we don't meet
I ask alongside all the best to god
You would remain well in your life.
May all your desires materialise according to your longing.

Yes, if you ever hear this poem of mine, Attempt to call me
around the same time. Then I will tell you more such poems
From the bottom of my heart.

1.30AM 06/05/2021

158. My Birthday

Came my birthday, Came my birthday,
Merely noted like self realizing day,
Nobody discern this laud day ,

Nobody have me to get it extol,
To whom I could glorify my day,
My spirit fell into profound dissatisfaction,

While half-day passed away,
No good tidings moved toward me yet,
From my beloved that may rely on,

My heed went to black clouds,
Who are floating on my head to wishing,
Who got me delusion like a black-eyes,

But justice of nature is everywhere,
Who thought about my blissful birthday,
Black clouds and breeze fill out the sky,

The trees are swaying with the wind
It seemed as if the leaves were applauding
Drizzling on way who get realized me birthday,

I seemed a preview of happiness,
Whose redolence strew around me,
Assorted birds greeted me by flapping around me.

12.21am January (20/07/2021)

159. My hopes crashed on the road

Only a little bit difference of our eyes,
As my eyes are Brown along with many hope
Whereas your black eyes are full of hopes too.

Exertion of our ways will always be stagger
Even though they need to confront cruel hindrances,
Yet Many times our eyes are demolished on such a path.

Splashes of whose bursts,
Where our blinking eyes frequently reveal
The hidden mystery at its core by promptly.

When your sight came to the court of my eyes
What'd more sight there and
Saw there a fortune brimming with love.

When my eyes are arrived at the threshold of your black eyes
They track down a vacant yard there
And it seems barren to love.

My hopes of dreams are many, But
The hope with which my eyes came to
The courtyard of your heart appeared to be false.

12.25AM 09/08/2019

160. Trodden way of love

I am whom there are none to know,
Even though I am a human being,
But i dwelt in the trodden ways,
So all here remain unknown.

Even though deserted fell down here, However
I saw a soul along stunning black eyes,
This is how I saw hustle rising in the forests,
That lying seemed to be known.

Lit of whose give bright to the untrodden paths,
However still whose routes are unclear
A view gets pierced by black-eyes,
And daylight gets into the night.

I seem to be withheld by a spy time,
It has kept me lost in life,
Even if I am waiting for it, my age is passing and,
Something has already passed.

She is known girl for me,
Whereas I am not for her,
But how long will I remain unknown.
Now keeps hope of any assurance of black eyes to this passing
soul.

11.20 22/08/2022

161. Let me sing of my love

She got retained in my heart as though the drops of downpour
had been engrossed in the sand.

She is as dear to me as the night loves moon's milky rays,

My life is flowing towards Her love like a perennial river,

Her glance has settled in my yard of eyes as the oceans into an
earth,

As if it were the name of a divine goddess, So my breath makes a
rosary of your name.

The confluence of my eyes with her black eyes resembles the
downpour stirred blossoms,

I can't survive without her, similar to a fish without water.

I wait for her to come like the animals in the African's desert wait
for the downpour.

I probe to perceive her like a maths puzzle whereas it doesn't.

That's why my love-laden poems don't stop singing my love songs
in her memory.

11.01PM 20/08/2022

162. Tree of black eyes

The rays of your black-eyes,
Planted a tree in my heart's yard,
whose roots have spread far and wide,
Whose journey is keeping on deepen,
whose branches are bent downwards with weight,

whose leaves never let it go bald,
As the fair is full of crowd revelry,
Whose noise never lets me sleep,
Where the wind blows forever,
Its dense shade does not allow the daylight to fall down.

My soul is lost in such darkness,
Under whose roots my body seems to me bereft of life,
It keeps to expect the love of princess's soul to divulge,
whose reflection merges into the universe,
Whose scent makes my nervous heart beat faster,

My soul is withering day by day in its shadow,
Please cut down this tree,
So that the courtyard of my heart can absorb the sunlight,
Otherwise life will block my breath, Thus
The coming days willn't be happiness on this yard,

Then strangers will mourn on this yard,
Please don't plant such a tree in someone else's yard.
However,
if you want to plant a tree,
Plant a tree that issues life to every soul.

3.46pm March (31/03/2020)

163. Slayer of soul

Your memory came suddenly,
And it stirred my heart.
It was like a cloud fell from the mountain
And it started raining in the valley.

As Inward feeling of harmony has been jumble,
As though the tranquillity of the valley has become unsound,
Such a heap of your recollections fell on the patio of my heart,
As a huge number of rocks from a mountain slide down to valley,

As soon as thunder lightning flashed in sky,
The people of the valley were aghast,
My face became numb as well,
Just like your black eyes that were flickering on my way.

As the water filled the valley
And the living souls drowned,
Since likewise your recollections inundated The patio of my
   heart,

Many lives have died
And carrying on to die,
Even my alone soul has perished
In this ocean of recollections.

10.45AM 23/03/2023

164. Then I wonder what to write about you?

I don't know what to write,
About my love for your hate
Or I Write your hate or write a declaration of my love,
Tell me, my dear,
What should I write?

whenever
I think of writing your beauty
Then a thought comes that I should write about your thinking
Then I stop and then
Then I think about what to write about you.

Many times
I think of writing about your beautiful black eyes,
But then many other thoughts delay
The writing of that thought.
Then I think what to write about you

Sometimes I like to write about your pink lips
After seeing the rose flowers,
Then when I smell the roses and
Then I forget to write,
Then I think about what to write about you.

Whenever I see white clouds in the blue sky.
I want to write about your milky colour
But when you come before me
I forgets to write,
Then I think about what to write about you.

So I don't know nothing, However
I have numerous thoughts regarding expounding on you,
Whereas , this skirmish of thoughts doesn't Allow me to compose
   anything,

Then I wonder what to write about you.

2.10 pm 18/07/2023

165. keys of love

Without wisdom,
The mind is foolish.
Like without the soul
The body is dust.

Without breath,
The body is an empty box,
Like without love
Heart is a useless trash heap.

Without your affection
My yard is dark
Like without the sun
The earth is dark.

Without me,
There is no joy in your yard.
Like without stars
There is no brightness in the sky.

Let us live together in the courtyard of love.
As the beams of the sun and moon live on earth.

4.30 PM 08/01/2024

166. Quiet Glimpse of our love

My love like a overwhelmed river
That is overflowing
From banks of my heart,

My sentiments touch you
Like the rays of sun
That kissing the earth at dawn

Glimpse of my eyes
Stays on you, like a peeping of
The moon's milky beams on earth.

Whisper of your charming beauty
Could be listen through
Your breathing.

Flow of your converse
Writes out a love way
At a blow randomly.

An asset of your black-eyes
Are balancing an obligation
On the way to my genuine romance.

Your quick steps push back my love
That assesses us sentiments on the love yard.
As a distance between us.

9.50pm 09/08/2022

167. Statement of Black Eyes

Too stunning black eyes descry as,
As black clouds floating in firmament,
As if they are set off to pour rain,
In which diverse birds are fluttering by sloppy,

As if these were waiting someone,
It looked like the ruins valley, In the lap of Whose Prosperous
     days are looking to
Under the fluttering shadow of them.

The only inner ray of hope was waking up,
To discover a decent way of life,
Which leads to the path of true love,
It tends to the longing soul,

No exertion is going in vain, In such valley
Each effort is stepping towards the lover,
As if her gaze is wandering tirelessly
Whose threshold is ever open to welcome his steps.

A dream soul seem to be ornate on threshold,
A true and right loving soul has her in,
who can make her wishes come true of life,
Only long lasting being Awaited by Her, who'll be able to bank on
     it.

1:42am 12/01/2020

168. Xylograph reprents artistry of love

I don't know why you don't like my love
But i am doing it tirelessly.
Like a butterfly that follows flowers at any time of day or night,
My love is following you.

Indeed, even those with eyes can't see
My flying affection like this.
However, those who have love in their hearts can feel my love,
Even if they are blind or dumb.

Indeed, even my companions will make fun of My silent love.
Yet such love will still inspire love even
In the hearts of my adversaries.

You won't believe my love,
I'm sure, with your black eyes.
However, I'm also sure that other young women
Will sympathy in this genuine romance of mine.

I additionally know that
Such love of mine is ruining my life.
Despite the fact that your such
Unbending contempt is most certainly helping my compositions.

2.50 PM 08/01/2023

169. Unreal love

Wind is like beloved of mine whose eyes black
Who is giving me breath constantly, So l love it very much.
When it kisses often on my lips
My parched lips sucked her gentle lips.

The sun seems to be my father
I'm asking him for gifts like my dad
First of all, I am asking for a fairy with like golden eyes
He has been nodding his head to me yet I don't have any idea
    when he will give it to me.

Earth is appeared to be my mom
It keeps preventing me from
The path of love that leads to my beloved's prompts.
She is stressed over her son's concern.

I wish to love my girlfriend wind forever
I always want to receive the warmth of my dad Sun's love at his
    feet.
And I wish to adore the feet of my mom earth daily.
Who gives me food on time to eat.

10.30 PM 08/01/2024

170. Wind teasing me

Today, the wind teased me again by calling your name

My feet are not touching the ground like the butterfly in a spring.

Thousands of emotions rivers have started streamed inside me

No matter how long it has been.
Then your black eyes are appearing like moon night

Still your stubborn stands like a Himalayan mountain in front of my love

But still I am sitting in the shelter of Mount Kailash in these Himalayas which has not yet been touchdown by anyone

But I still seem my love is the eighth wonder of the world

But now what should I tell the wind?

Who is shouting on our names as you and mine.

You may not hear it shouting, but my ears are being deaf.

9.15 PM 10/01/2024

171. Golden Eyes

I'm a tree under a foreboding shadows
Whose shadow stolen the spring of my life
Life was slipping away day by day
Nothing was looking for a way to live in such darkness.

Still, I didn't give up hope of living like a bedridden patient
The breaths are also coming out by counting
The mind was longing for the light of the sun
Like a labourer living in a mine.

As soon as the rays of the golden eyes of
The sun fell on these shadows
The black eyes of these dark shadows
That have been watching over me began to disappear.

The one who saves lives is God in human form.
I wish to live in the courtyard of such blooming light
I want to thank you for such golden eyes.
Who gave me hope for another new life.

Presently I'm living in such blossoming light
That came into my life, That gleamed me.
Those eyes love me and converse with me through their glowing
    warmth.
I was already looking for such a life of illuminating sun.

5.40 PM 08/01/2024